THE PRINCIPLES AND PRACTICE OF

THE PRINCIPLES AND PRACTICE OF

UNDERSTANDING THE PURPOSE OF GIVING
OSIEN SIBANDA

SIBANDA
PUBLISHING

A catalogue record for this book is available from the British Library.

Published in the United Kingdom by Sibanda Publishing.

ISBN: 978-0-9561175-1-9

Printed & bound in the UK by J F Print Ltd., Sparkford, Somerset.

Acknowledgements

One notable author observed that everything we accomplish in life is a synergistic product of many people who have contributed to what we are and what we do. I am no different, nor is this book. A number of people have encouraged me and helped me throughout this project and some have quizzed me on my intentions as I wrote, resulting in what I consider to be a balanced presentation of my thoughts and observations. I am eternally grateful for whatever support I received.

There are those who deserve mention in their effort and the first is my wife, Fatima. Thank you for the gift of life we share together.

To my daughters, Lebo and Ayanda, thank you for the life you bring to our home. We would not be what we are without you.

To my late dad, Ariel, who did his best to raise me under the harsh and cruel system that never gave him a chance to compete in the market place like anybody else. I cannot wait to see him in glory and salute him for the effort he made despite the obstacles he faced.

To my mother, Alice Mathayi, words can not express what a wonderful mother you are. With no education at all you took on the world and found your place among the elite, and you still are. You gave your life and energies for others to attain what you could not due to your circumstances. Thank God for the warrior in you. You did not allow your limitations to affect your offspring. You love all your children the same, you fought for justice and equity, and you truly are a Proverbs 31 woman. God bless you, Mama!

To all my brothers and sisters, thank you for the lessons we shared, both negative and positive. They have helped to shape me into who I am today and I am eternally grateful.

To Uncle Richard and his wife, Sofie, thank you for the experience you gave me from 1972 to 1977. Working in your fields and looking after your sheep, goats, donkeys and cattle has helped me understand certain aspects of life and the Bible even better, thank you!

The pastors I have worked with, both the understanding and caring ones who have helped me discover my potential, and those who were challenging and difficult, who helped polish my character, thank you. May you continue the good work.

To those whose stories I have used, thank you. I learnt some valuable lessons from you which have saved me and hopefully many more from repeating your mistakes. It can be all too easy to judge when someone makes a mistake, but sometimes it is through these mistakes that we learn, both the person who made them and others close by, observing. I realise that most of those mistakes were made from a position in which you were doing the best of what you knew, but now being more enlightened we can spot the errors which will, I hope, help future generations of leaders not to fall into the same trap. So, I am grateful to God for you and for the freedom I have to communicate those challenges for the benefit of others.

To the church community and brethren I have lived with in various churches in different countries I have been to, thank you for each and every opportunity that has helped me to be who I am today.

A special thanks goes to Adzira Thahal, for being the first person to read my original manuscript and critique it so objectively, and helping me give it shape and a better flow. God bless you.

CONTENTS

INTRODUCTION

Principles are frequently misunderstood in many Christian circles today. A lot of teachings talk of living by principles but don't actually explain what they mean by that. There are principles of management, principles of education, principles of finance... and so on. And in most eras of history we have been taught to follow principles if we are to succeed.

What then are principles?

A principle is a rule or code of conduct. It is a fundamental law that helps you to conduct yourself in a particular field or discipline. When it comes to giving, certain fundamental laws describe or guide us into understanding the purposes of giving. Why do people give to one another? Why give to other organisations and people in need? The answers to these questions are found in the fundamental laws or principles, and these will never change. The most fundamental principle about giving is that it is not a human attribute, it originates with God! *"For God so loved the world that He gave his only Son..."*

The dictionary defines giving as "to present voluntarily and without expecting compensation". We do this all the time in one way or the other. The key thing in giving is to remember that this presentation or giving is done voluntarily or willingly. For us to understand this code of conduct, it will be helpful to look at the people in the Bible and try to determine their reasons and motivation for giving. There in the Bible, in addition to the principles, we have the practices of giving, which will show us how different people practised giving throughout many generations. This practice is usually based on fundamental laws – the principles. Understanding these will determine how we put them into practice. And how this is done will differ from people to people and time to time.

Principles are the road map to guide us in a particular task. They give us a structure that explains what we do. When it comes to giving, compassion and love will be the passion that helps us stay focused on giving. We give because we love. We give because we are compassionate.

This road map will enable you to properly practise the principles of giving and consequently give us pleasure in doing so, because it is more blessed to give than to receive. That is the reason John D. Rockefeller Jr., the wealthy American philanthropist and expert in industrial relations advocates that we should think of giving not as a duty but as a privilege.[1] This can only happen when we understand the reason and purpose for giving, which is to bless others. Maya Angelou, the Black African-American poet and author once said: "I have found that among its other benefits, giving liberates the soul of the giver."[2] Giving is good for you. As you learn to be free from the bondage of possessions, you are free to share what you have.

The challenge we have today is that prosperity teaching has confused giving with working. Giving is now being taught as a means to achieve wealth and success. However, on careful study of the Bible, I have discovered that this is not the case. The results and focus of the two are miles apart. They are different. Working brings wealth and substance into your life. It increases your assets. That is the purpose of working. Giving, on the other hand, diminishes those assets as you share them with other people. This is how it should work.

This misunderstanding has led to many believers giving a lot with the hope of attaining a harvest. This book therefore seeks to explain the principles and practices of giving from Old Testament times through to New Testament times, and the difference between the principles and the practices. It seeks to prove that giving was not at all meant to bring you a harvest and to prosper you, although giving should be central to our daily Christian lives as it is an outward expression of inner love and concern.

There are many books and opinions about giving, prosperity, wealth and success, and the Bible is unquestionably one of them. Yet it is clear that financial prosperity does not only come about through reading the pages of books and learning from people's opinions. Nor does it come just through following the examples of others, although their testimonies may serve as good motivation and encouragement. Prosperity involves much more than that, and people prosper in different ways as long as they follow the principles that lead to financial success.

But it must be made clear right from the outset that giving alone was never designed to make one rich, no matter who preaches it! While the message of the Bible is clear in many instances, there are a number of passages that are difficult to interpret and this results in teachings that confuse many people, especially in the area of giving and receiving, and sowing and reaping a harvest.

The message of prosperity and examples of prosperous people in the Bible are numerous and span through many generations, but the question is – are we to imitate them so that we can prosper like them?

We must understand that prosperity in itself is neither wrong nor a sin. According to *Proverbs 28:25*, God actually promises prosperity to those who trust in Him: *"He who trusts in the Lord will prosper."* But it will not just 'drop in our lap'. We must do our part. When Joshua is promised prosperity in *Joshua 1:8*, it is conditional: *"This Book of the Law shall not depart from your mouth, but you shall meditate in it day and night, that you may observe to do according to all that is written in it. For then you will make your way prosperous, and then you will have good success" (NKJV)*. The promise given to Joshua depended on him keeping the law, and it was he

(Joshua) who would make his own way prosperous – God wouldn't just do it for him.

It is also important to realise that although there are many prosperous individuals mentioned in the Bible, there are many more wealthy and prosperous people who never even made it into the pages of the Bible. How then did they prosper without any knowledge of the Bible, if the Bible is the only basis of prosperity? Even around us today, there are more successful and prosperous non-believers than believers.

We must not limit our understanding of prosperity to money and to the few individuals recorded in the Bible, as the Bible only focused on one group of people – the Jews, and those who had an interaction of some kind with them. There were many more prosperous people that are not mentioned in the Bible, and some rich people who do appear in the Bible did not make their wealth through the wisdom of the Bible. The Queen of Sheba is one such example. When she, a foreigner, first appears in the pages of the Bible, she is already a very prosperous and wealthy woman. As *1 Kings 10:2* says: *"Arriving at Jerusalem with a very great caravan— with camels carrying spices, large quantities of gold, and precious stones— she came to Solomon..."* And these were just the gifts that she was offering to Solomon.

You don't need Bible knowledge to be prosperous, it would seem. For us therefore to make a fuss about the Bible and prosperity as though the Bible is the only instrument of prosperity is falling short of understanding its purpose. The

Bible serves as a moderator to a society that is already either prosperous or poor. It shows us the way to a relationship with our Creator and how He wants us to live together with understanding and compassion while here on earth. As *Proverbs 19:17* states: *"He who is kind to the poor lends to the Lord, and he will reward him for what he has done."* Who would not want to know that the Lord owes him something? *Proverbs 28:27* also teaches that he who gives to the poor will be rewarded. But *Proverbs 19:17* is a typical example of how the Bible encourages us to live well together. The Bible acknowledges that not everyone will have enough money or food, hence the importance of giving.

We must realise that material prosperity does nothing to make one holy, and it is definitely not a recipe for Christ-likeness. To consider it above the salvation of souls is to malign the sacrifice of the cross. Therefore we must not be tempted to focus on it; prosperity is only temporal, even though it makes life comfortable and easier. Nowhere in the pages of Scripture is the temporal and material elevated in importance above the spiritual! Instead, souls are to be our goal. Therefore when the Bible talks about prosperity it is not referring only to financial prosperity.

When Moses, the author of the first five books of the Bible, was born in Egypt, the Egyptians were already wealthy and rich, according to Exodus. How then did this happen before they had the Bible, if we are to take our cue on prosperity from the Bible alone? What about the many unbelievers who are prosperous today – how do they do it without the

Bible? The way to prosperity is apparent and can be chartered without the Bible – it seems!

But the Bible does explain how to create prosperity in a way that honours God.

Chapter One

THE ENIGMA
AROUND WEALTH

We live in a world of great contrasts, with the rich and powerful on one hand, and the poor and weak on the other. There is very little in-between! This raises a lot of questions about the disparity of life in general.

Two types of battle typically unfold, with one group seeking to survive, and the other to consolidate its hold on wealth. Consequently, the worst people among the rich tend to use those without wealth as their servants, paying such people just enough to remain dependent on them while making a lot out of them. The worst of the poor, on the other hand, take every possible opportunity to steal from the wealthy in order to live comfortably, or try to do as little work as possible as a way of protest against oppression.

In some communities, especially in Africa, the supernatural is engaged to try and break the impasse of poverty. The mystery around wealth and how it is obtained is intense and indeed surprising. Two purveyors of the supernatural are usually involved – fortune tellers and witch doctors. Fortune tellers offer guidance in finding an advantage over competitors. Witch doctors, although poor themselves, claim that the concoctions they prescribe make one rich. One only wonders how they don't get wealthy themselves if what they claim is true. This is indeed a mystery!

I know of instances where families have been advised by witch doctors to murder a loved one or a close relative in order to activate the spirit of success and wealth – and some people have done it. At one shop I know, the workers uncovered a human hand in the freezer. This had been prescribed by a witch doctor who claimed that the hand would continually call customers into the shop and thus help them make a lot of money. Many more stories are told of certain body parts that work as a draw card for customers and innocent lives have been taken just for the pursuit of wealth.

According to a documentary programme in one medical university in South Africa, the person in charge of the morgue was caught selling body parts to aspiring and practising business people. The Star, one of South Africa's leading newspapers, carried an article that says some people are even smoking vulture brains in order to see opportunities for business. Some even claim that due to a vulture's good eyesight, eating or smoking its dried brain helps one see the winning numbers of the lottery. Vultures are sold at up to £200, just for their brain. This puts pressure on the population of the innocent bird that is now hunted in order to help people get rich. It is ridiculous!

Some churches are just as misleading in their teaching on wealth. While they will not murder, or buy a human hand or a child's eye to enhance their chances of prosperity, they do promise people wealth and riches if they go through all sorts of shenanigans in order to make a financial breakthrough.

A lot of poor families' suffering is made even worse by trying to find a shortcut to escape from their poverty. Desperate people tend to fall into the trap of believing anything that promises to ease their burden in the quickest possible way. I know this only too well, as this was a battle my family of 15 (including our parents) fought when I was a child. We fought to survive, and we sought wealth in which ever way promised to meet our need.

My mother's eldest sister was a witch doctor, and at her death the 'spirit' went into my mother's last born sister. To be accepted in the family, this 'spirit' promised everybody wealth, claiming this was the mandate it had been given by our great ancestors. The message was that our ancestors were now about to help us attain financial freedom and wealth, despite the fact that they themselves died poor. Yet there was so much faith in the idea of assistance from a source beyond human effort that we fervently believed it. The 'spirit' narrated my mother's entire history as she and her brothers knew it, and because of desperation and a new promise of wealth, we all welcomed it with great enthusiasm and anticipation, and submitted to it by various weird rituals, never questioning how this wealth would come.

Sacrifices and feasts were made in exactly the way this 'spirit' demanded, but no wealth arrived. This put the family deeper and deeper into problems, as we kept on spending the little we had in the hope of striking it rich one day. I for one thought I would in due course stumble across a bag of money somewhere as I walked along the crowded streets. I never once thought: "Why on earth would someone leave behind a bag of money for me to pick up?"

Not one of us considered a job or a business of some kind as a way of fulfilling our desire for wealth. We watched our neighbours prosper, selling goods at street corners and shops, but we were so focused on the promise of supernatural intervention that we never did much to help ourselves. Although we did a bit of selling of the clothes and jerseys my mother and sister would sew and knit, we never did it at a wider scale because we were not business-minded. After all, our ancestors were busy preparing a bumper harvest for us! It's only now that I realise that we had a great opportunity to become business people as we sold those clothes then, but because of our ignorance we did not seize the moment.

The Bible is right to say people perish for lack of vision or knowledge (*Hosea 4:6*). We lacked both! We would swindle Mum and steal some of the money from the proceeds of her efforts. Sometimes we would claim that we gave people discount when in fact we used the money for our own things. A lot of times that money would be spent on sweets or gambling. Precious time and resources were lost in the hope of miraculous provision, but it never came. In our desperation, we chose to blindly trust in a lie that got us deeper and deeper into trouble, and the sad thing is that we were not the only ones. This still happens today. And not just in the world, but also in the Church, as I mentioned before, where the truth is supposed to be taught.

The problems caused by poverty and wealth have contributed to repression and torment in the world as we know it today. This is not unique to the unchurched. Christians can also find themselves on either side of the wealth equation, yet they are provided for by the same God. Some wealthy ministers ascribe their success to obedience to God and to sowing on good ground, while the poor still wait on God for their turn. Or at least continue giving until their seed falls on good ground as well. Both turn to the Scriptures, yet the results are different. How the differences come to be is a mystery. Why God prospers one and not the other while loving them both is a question only He can answer (though He clearly does love both equally, as *"God does not show favouritism"* – *Romans 2:11*).

Some people see wealth as a blessing, a sign of obedience to the teachings of Scripture. But this idea can put pressure on individuals that have not yet received this blessing, and can cause individuals to take desperate measures to gain wealth, often to the detriment of many, as I experienced in my early years. The truth is that the Bible never speaks of a total elimination of poverty, but it does stress the need to take care of the poor, defend them and give them the opportunity to improve their lot.

Jesus clearly said that we will always have the poor with us. But this is not a licence to oppress and manipulate them. If poverty is always going to exist, then the question is how those with wealth can best share it with those without, so that all might live well.

Today, in many parts of the world, we find numerous government ministers living in untold luxury with expensive lifestyles and massive cars. They live in houses with too many rooms for them to use, while the cost of upkeeping that home could feed an entire village in a developing country. All this is paid for by the taxpayer, who they claim to be serving and whose interests they claim to have at heart. They campaign for votes and promise to change the lives of the poor. Eventually, the lives they change are their own, using their influence and power to enrich themselves while the poor remain the same.

Sadly, some gospel ministers are no different! They also claim to be shepherds, called by God to feed His lambs, just as Peter was instructed by the Good Shepherd to feed His lambs (*John 21:15*). It is indeed a paradox that many shepherds are feeding themselves more than the sheep they were commanded to feed.

These ministers claim to understand how to tap into the promises of God about wealth. Sometimes it is their sowing that brings the harvest, so they say. They claim to be givers, and this makes them rich and wealthy. What does this translate to? Whoever wants to prosper like them must give like them. But it is interesting who receives and benefits from those gifts and who determines how they are used. The shepherds, of course!

We have begun to see the Church getting caught up in worldly behaviour, with some leaders using the Scriptures to justify their greed, insensitivity and love of money. This puts a lot of pressure on the followers as they seek to be like their leaders. Lots of money is collected from unsuspecting churchgoers, who give with the hope of getting more, as they follow the teachings that promise them results.

In too many churches the amount of money used to sustain church ministers and ministries is far greater than the budget to support the poor and needy. What then is the purpose of the church? Many churches run like businesses, with their pastors sometimes earning more than some company executives, yet they are considered to be non-profit making organisations.

It is indeed a wonder how they continue to raise such vast sums of money. Obviously the offering bowl is the channel, but the question is, how do they get their followers to continue giving to their cause? The promise and hope of a harvest one day is the bait, supported by numerous testimonies to serve as motivational traps. In such circumstances, it is easy to understand why many people shun modern Pentecostal churches and their message of prosperity, mistakenly branding wealth itself as evil and the possession of wealth as essentially bad.

The contradiction between the frugal life of Jesus Christ and some of His richer servants today also raises question marks over the prosperity message. Is this really God's way of prosperity? The same contrast could be made between prosperity teachers and the apostle Paul and most of his followers. His encouragement was plain and simple: *"Follow my example, as I follow the example of Christ" (1 Corinthians 11:1).* Christ's lifestyle was simple and open for all to see and emulate. So the question then becomes, how can we be prosperous in the way God wants us to be? God will not manipulate or favour one above another. He is a righteous God, His Word says. So we need to discover God's way of understanding prosperity, using the Scriptures, and, of course, our common sense!

Chapter Two

WHAT IS THE PROSPERITY MESSAGE?

T he prosperity message bases its teaching on the harvest which is promised to those who give money to the causes of Christ. This giving is described as sowing seed. The result is referred to as the harvest, which comes supernaturally – by way of a miracle. The giver is promised a harvest proportional to what they sow; this is taken from a number of scriptural references that need to be looked at objectively... *"A man reaps what he sows... Ask and it will be given to you... And my God will meet all your needs according to his glorious riches in Christ Jesus" (Galatians 6:7; Matthew 7:7; Philippians 4:19).* The idea presented is that you give in order to get more – GIVING TO GET. It sounds like a Christian lottery or, as someone put it, the saints' stock market! "God needs your money He will provide 30, 60 and 100-fold returns." Some messages like these, and the messengers who deliver them, as Clay Sikes rightly observed, sound more like stock traders than preachers.[1]

He states: "The abuses I have personally witnessed have the same results – skinning of the sheep, while certain beneficiaries (the shepherds) grow fatter. I have seen life savings, children's college funds and retirement savings emptied into the coffers of church leaders and TV evangelists."[2]

The 30, 60, and 100-fold has seldom happened for most who have bought into this lie, not because God does not want to bless, but because the order and motive is wrong. God is a God of order and He will not bless disorder.

Over the years, I have come to question this message of sowing and reaping from the perspective of a lot of these modern-day preachers. An in-depth study of the Bible, and also the practicalities of sowing and harvesting, has made me realise that today's Pentecostal teaching on giving is misguided, and the sowers are getting ripped off! It is definitely not God's way to prosper. *Proverbs 18:19* teaches that prosperity comes through work, not miracles. The opposite is also true concerning poverty. *"He who tills his land will have plenty of bread. But he who follows frivolity will have poverty enough!"*

Prosperity by definition means to achieve economic success or well-being and enjoy vigorous and healthy growth. This is acceptable. It is different from extravagance, which means exceeding the limits of reason or necessity, or a lack of moderation, balance and restraint!

I once listened to a prominent minister brag about how 'loaded' he was and that he wanted people to have money because money and peace are related. Money would therefore bring them peace, he claimed. What he did not tell people is how he gets loaded. It would have been much better if he had told his audience how he makes his money. He simply claims that it is because he is a giver. This is not true as *Proverbs 28:19* has just warned us. He writes books and sells them to you, and most of his sermons are on CD and he sells them to you. When he speaks at conferences, he gets paid. Not that this is wrong, but that is how he is making money. That is how he gets loaded! This is how he tills his land. He is using his gifts and talents to make a living, which is good.

You must also have a way of making money other than just giving. You must give from what you have. You don't make money by giving. There is no scripture to this effect and basic economics will not sustain this teaching. This is where the problem of the prosperity gospel lies. They want to make you think you prosper by just giving. This is far from the truth. Look for something to do that will raise revenue! Find your own land and till it according to *Proverbs 28:19*. Your security lies in your power to produce something, not in giving alone. Having that power to produce wealth is what makes you prosperous. Be a creator of wealth – don't just expect to be a receiver of wealth because you have given in the offering or to some miserable beggar. Wealth is made not received as many gospel teachers say. *"But remember the Lord your God, for it is He who gives you power to get wealth…"* *(Deuteronomy 8:18).* Why would you need power to get wealth if it was merely received just by giving? The word "get" in the Hebrew in this case implies doing or to make. The word power on the other hand speaks of vigour, not just prayer power or powerful prayers. Wealth is made. God does not just give us wealth but the power and vigour to make it and it is up to us to use that power.

"If you have money, you will have peace," claimed the prominent minister I mentioned earlier. Which peace is he talking about? One of the richest men on earth understood that money does not bring peace. John Rockefeller said: "Even the poorest man I know is the man who has nothing but money." He went on to say, "I have made many millions, but they have brought me no happiness." Henry Ford adds to this in his popular statement, "I was happier doing a mechanic's job," meaning there is more stress and anxiety in having more resources than less as observed by W. H. Vanderbilt, "The care of $200 million is enough to kill anyone. There is no pleasure in it." It is therefore misleading to teach that money brings peace although we would be foolish to think that wealth is not necessary. It is the way to obtain it that is an issue here.

Jesus made a distinction between His peace and the peace of the world. In *John 14:27* He says: *"Peace I leave with you; my peace I give you. I do not give to you as the world gives."* Peace therefore can be understood from God's perspective and from the perspective of the world – and they are two different things. Saying money gives peace is definitely a worldly perspective.

I know a friend who was an avid supporter of this teaching and he gave away most of his earnings, to the extent that he was left with nothing. Friends would have to bail him out until pay day came round again. He was a very faithful Christian, but very poor. He could hardly take care of himself. The Bible severely reprimands those who will not take care of their household: *"If anyone does not provide for his relatives, and especially for his immediate family, he has denied the faith and is worse than an unbeliever" (1 Timothy 5:8).*

If anyone was going to benefit from the results of the prosperity gospel's teaching on giving it was my friend, but alas! His story was miserable. Most unbelievers used his lifestyle to illustrate why they believed Christianity was evil. The motive and reason for giving must be right if God is to bless us! If we continue giving to get, the Bible says we will not profit from it. *1 Corinthians 13:3* says: *"If I give all I possess to the poor and surrender my body to the flames, but have not love, I gain nothing."* Judge for yourself, then, why this teaching of giving to get is flawed!

Chapter Three

WHERE DID IT ALL GO WRONG?

I n his thesis, 'Examining the Biblical Support for Christians with Regard to Prosperity', Terrance Irwin points to a worrying observation by David Biema and Jeff Chu about a developing philosophy in some of today's Pentecostal churches regarding success and prosperity.[1]

They noted that for several decades this philosophy has been penetrating the Pentecostal wing of Christianity (which a cautious estimate numbers at 200 million people worldwide). It seems to turn the Gospel message about prosperity on its head, especially when it is closely compared to the words and lifestyles of Jesus and the early apostles. The turning point in the departure from a balanced biblical view of prosperity was when the prosperity teaching literature shifted from what Steven Covey, the author of the popular Seven Habits of Highly Effective People calls, the Character Ethic to the Personality Ethic.[2] This was the beginning of trouble.

Known under a variety of names – Seed Faith, Sowing and Reaping, Giving and Receiving, Name It and Claim It or Claim it and Have It – this new prosperity theology emphasised a God who does not want His children to be poor. It is based on a number of verses that need closer scrutiny and sound exegesis.

Steven Covey, also alludes to this observation after studying the prosperity literature for the past 200 years. He noticed that for the last 50 years or so, much of the success literature that has permeated society has been superficial. It is filled with social image consciousness, easy techniques and quick fixes that apply social band-aids and asprin to acute problems. It sometimes appears to solve them temporarily, but leaves the underlying chronic problems untouched, to fester and resurface time and time again.[3]

Covey calls this the Personality Ethic. In this approach, success becomes more of a function of personality, public image, attitude and behaviour. It is the celebrity syndrome! Get popular and rich overnight, if you have what it takes. The philosophy is: "Your attitude determines your altitude, and whatever the mind of man can conceive and believe it can achieve." This is precisely what Terrance Irwin termed a worrying phenomenon,[4] as it teaches that whatever you claim becomes yours. While this can be true to a certain extent, teaching it as a doctrine for prosperity because of the experiences and testimonies of other people becomes dangerous. On closer scrutiny the personality approach is clearly manipulative, and even deceptive in the way it encourages people to use techniques to get other people to give them what they want.

On the other hand, 100 years before this tendency, teachings on prosperity were sound and very practical. The foundation of success and prosperity then was on things like integrity, humility, fidelity, temperance, courage, justice, patience, hard work, simplicity and modesty. Covey calls this approach the Character Ethic. It teaches that there are basic principles of effective living, and that people can only experience true success and enduring happiness as they learn to integrate these principles into their basic character and lifestyle.[5]

This shift from the Character Ethic to the Personality Ethic occurred shortly after World War Two, and from then on, reference to the Character Ethic became lip service; the basic thrust was quick-fix influence techniques, power strategies, communication skills and positive attitudes. Covey gives a strong warning about the danger of focussing on techniques rather than principles. He warns: "To focus on technique is like cramming your way through school."[6] You might sometimes get by and even get good results, but if you don't pay the price day in and day out, you never achieve true mastery of the subjects you study.

In fact, it's more like trying to cram your way through the farming year, he jokes: "To forget to plant in the spring, play all summer and then cram in the fall to bring in the harvest."[7] The farm is a natural system and the price must be paid and the process followed if one is to benefit from it.

This 'paying the price' concept was the teaching 200 years ago and it worked. This is precisely Irwin's concern and observation, as the new teaching tends to sway people away from the principles that used to sustain them. It's more like removing the ancient landmarks that our fathers set up in direct contradiction to the advice given in *Proverbs 22:28: "Do not move an ancient boundary stone set up by your forefathers."*

If God does not want us to be poor, why then did He allow His Son to be poor? The answer is that Jesus became poor so that we, through His poverty, may become rich. But what does the Bible mean by poverty in this case?

Jesus talks about the poor that we will always have with us, and He also talks about the poor in spirit, who He says are blessed *(Matthew 5:3)*. Where do we draw the line between those who are supposedly destined to be poor and the poor who must work their way up through sowing and the harvest?

Although the prosperity message first blazed to public attention in the days of Jim Bakker and Jimmy Swaggart according to Irwin,[8] it had already started showing its head in the 1800s, and John Wesley spoke strongly against it in some of his sermons in the early days of Methodism. Wesley noted that in the old days of Methodism, the people were poor. But he observed that as the church grew, many Methodists became rich and wealthy and they decreased in godliness. It seemed to him, the more the Methodists had, the less they loved the Lord. He complained that too few preachers preached against the sin of loving money, which he believed hindered revival.[9]

This prosperity message and attitude continued to grow quickly and few in the Pentecostal Movement itself seemed to challenge it. It now forms one of the most aggressive and grossly ambiguous doctrines of the modern-day Pentecostal message: Giving and Receiving. This message promises a bigger harvest, the bigger the seed that is sown. The seed, for many, is the money they give in their offerings in church. Giving, for these people, is mainly viewed in terms of a church setting, where the funds are directed to the 'man of God' – the church's pastor.

Nowadays the message has been polished by a new group of wealth-conscious preachers, making it appealing to many Christians across the globe who are desperate to reap great harvests from effortless sowing. Interviewing one such pastor about his life, Randy Alcorn was shocked by his answer, which claimed that God does not want all His children in economy class; He wants some of them in first class.[10] Really?! Did God actually say that? How then does God select those to live in untold luxury if He does not show favouritism? *(See Romans 2:11.)* Does God speak like that? Most of the first class this pastor was talking about is funded by those he considers to be in economy!

Another very prominent voice of the prosperity gospel had a shocking interpretation of the Bible. At 80 years of age, he still believed that God wants pastors to prosper in order for their followers to have enough faith to prosper as well.[11] This is not God's way to prosperity. People who believe this have given to make sure the pastor gets rich first, so that they can then have their turn! Giving then ceases to be an act of worship and it becomes questionable who the Church is now giving to – man or God? The motive is drastically wrong.

Why must the faith of the congregation be benchmarked by that of the pastor, as far as finances are concerned? Why must it be measured by wealth and possessions? Is this not manipulation and daylight robbery? The Scriptures show that this type of servanthood is the opposite of the God these pastors claim to serve. *Mark 10:45* states that this same God sent His Son into the world, not to be served but to serve. But these ministers choose to hide behind the name of God to acquire wealth.

Prosperity preachers have claimed that if you want God to supply your financial needs, then give money... and if your need is not money but something else, let your money represent it. If seeds produce after their kind, how can the seed of money now represent a harvest of a different kind? This is all twisted faith based on a twisted doctrine by twisted preachers in a twisted world. It is tantamount to theft.

What is the seed and harvest?

In *Luke chapter 8*, Jesus tells a parable of a farmer who went out to sow. He makes it clear in this case that the seed that is planted is the Word of God. Seeds always produce after their kind, according to Genesis.

This principle will never change. The Word of God in this case has the potential to produce godliness in our hearts when we believe and choose to obey it. In this respect it is different to the natural seed, which has no choice but to produce after its kind. The seed of the Word must be believed because it's not a natural seed, but a spiritual seed and the law of spiritual seeds is that they work by faith and obedience. They must be believed; again, this is how God chose it to work.

What does this mean for prosperity teaching? Well, the problem is that Bible teachers often make analogies with the law of the seed because this physical process is already understood by congregations and so it makes a good illustration, for people to get the point of a message. In Jesus' example, the seed represented the Word of God, but the seed can represent almost anything, depending on what point we are seeking to put across.

There is no problem with that as long as our intentions are made clear to the listeners. But if the seed and the harvest terminology is always taught as referring to money, it becomes a problem. In *Luke 8*, Jesus' seed was the Word and the harvest was people. Why? Because the Word was sent to save people, or re-direct them from their wrong ways, through instruction of the Word.

When it comes to finances, a lot of our modern-day teachings have mixed up the real meaning of the seed and harvest. This has had a dramatic impact on our attitudes to giving and has opened the door for some people to exploit unsuspecting believers.

In the Old Testament, sowing and reaping were understood in their practical light and that meant hard work, sweat and effort – using one's hands. This involved day-to-day work in the field and this is how the people of old sustained their lives. Their giving and offerings came from the proceeds of hard labour and diligence in tilling the land, looking after sheep and cattle or whatever way one chose to provide for one's needs.

God wants to bless the work of our hands, according to *Deuteronomy 14:29* and *Deuteronomy 28:12* (in the present day the work of our hands is equivalent to our job). Out of the proceeds of this work came the tithe, to thank God for playing His part as the provider of the harvest. God's part must not be confused with our part. God brings the rain on time at various developmental stages of the crops, and it maintains the soil He has given us for growing our food. God also sustains the seasons, exactly as He promised just after the Flood *(Genesis 8:28)*.

The tithe therefore was an acknowledgement that while people till the land and sow the seed into the ground, the mystical miracle of turning it into a plant that then yields fruit is something only God can do. The land belongs to Him; He created it: *"The earth is the Lord's, and all its fullness, the world and those who dwell therein" (Psalm 24:1, NKJV).*

Many modern Pentecostal teachings equate an individual's financial offering with a seed planted to yield fruit, but when you really compare this with the words of the Bible, you find they are two different things. To put it plainly, your seed is the natural ability or skills given to you by God. You sow this seed by working or applying what God has given you to produce, to learn, to create or to even think. The proceeds, i.e. the pay you get after applying this seed, is your harvest. Obviously most of us do not own fields as people of old did, so our sustenance is from our jobs. If you do not sow a seed, and tend the plant, you don't get a harvest. In the same way, if you do not use your skills and work, you do not get paid.

Now, this means that your offering is your acknowledgement of the harvest, not a means to get a harvest! What you give is not your seed. Through giving the offering we engage with God out of a heart of obedience, gratitude and worship. We don't earn our salary from giving to Him, we give to Him out of the salary we have already earned.

So, the only way you can reap a harvest is by planting and tending to your seed. In other words, the only way you will get money and prosper is if you use your God-given abilities, skills and talents to work and be productive. There are no short cuts. Prayer is not designed to bring wages at the end of each month for a whole year. It may at some stage, when necessary, but teaching people to depend on it to do so is folly. Why ask God to do for you what He has already enabled you to do for yourself? Why ask God to do for you what your neighbour is already doing without God?!

Rather, be humble and ask him to teach you, or you will be praying for a long time. Some things in life are learned, and unless you are prepared to go through that process you will never prosper.

This is not a new, radical way of thinking, but is something that God put in place right from the word go, and I will now show you this, using a few examples from the Bible.

Wisdom, hard work and forward thinking

Let's go back to look at the story of Joseph. *Genesis 41:33 (KJV)* states: *"Now therefore let Pharaoh look out a man discreet and wise, and set him over the land of Egypt."* The land was about to get into a season of drought and famine, and the solution to this problem lay in a man. Not an ordinary man but a man who was discerning and wise. A wise person is a clever person, an intelligent, sensible and prudent person.

The opposite of wisdom is foolishness. Foolishness does not plan for the future, which is how, unfortunately, many Christians tend to choose to live today because of their understanding of prosperity. The word "discreet", on the other hand, is about being tactful, circumspect, discerning, cautious and careful.

Most believers do not apply this when they do their sowing in response to preachers. They are not careful where to place their money, and in the end they lose out and may turn away from God. Not everything that has God's name has the God of that name.

Prosperity requires diligence and tact. Farmers are diligent master planners who understand the seasons well. The Bible talks of the *"men of Issachar, who understood the times and knew what Israel should do" (1 Chronicles 12:32).* Those were the men David needed to accomplish his mission successfully. Prosperity and good harvests don't come to lazy people. You must be industrious and ready to try something new.

As soon as Joseph was given the responsibility to prepare for the hard task ahead, he did not sit on his laurels and wait for the Lord to show him a strategy in a dream, despite God speaking to him before in dreams. He literally travelled throughout the land of Egypt *(Genesis 41:46)*, familiarising himself with the people, his new position and the land, in preparation for the harvest. He was learning his new field of responsibility. He could have studied it from books but he chose the painful way of experiencing first hand, by being there. There was work to be done and it had to be planned for and systems had to be put in place. No harvest comes without hard work, otherwise it is not a harvest.

For the following seven years Joseph put his plans into action and co-ordinated the storage of the harvest into large silos. These must have been new silos that had to be designed, because no previous storage facilities could contain enough food to cater for a whole nation and outsiders for seven years.

Proverbs 6:10-11 reads: *"A little sleep, a little slumber, a little folding of the hands to rest – and poverty will come on you like a*

43

bandit and scarcity like an armed man.." Armed bandits don't signify something good! They destroy, and so does laziness and pride. Some people are poor because they are too lazy to think, too lazy to work and even too lazy to ask at times. Sometimes we don't have simply because we do not ask. When the Bible says ask and it shall be given to you, it does not only mean to ask from God; we can ask from other people as well.

Proverbs 6:6-8 states that the ant takes care of itself. It does so by understanding the seasons that have been set. Ants know that if they sit back during the harvest until all of it is picked up by others, they would starve in the winter when they cannot venture out of their burrows. Understanding the ant's operations is considered wisdom by the Scriptures. There is no such thing as sitting back and waiting for God to move on our behalf. He has already done so by providing seed to the sower and bringing rain at the right time. And by giving us a healthy body so we can work! Get down to work or buy and sell something, or offer to clear your neighbour's yard. There is always something to do if you look around, think and ask God to show you.

Prosperity in the Old Testament came through work; doing nothing was frowned upon! No one prayed for a harvest. They prayed for rain, as this was God's part, as was the case with Elijah in 1 Kings. People worked hard in order to possess and protect the harvest. That is precisely the reason why Jesus taught them to pray that there would be enough labourers to reap the spiritual harvest. There can be no harvest without workers to bring it in.

Everyone who listened to Jesus and His parables knew and understood the seasons and their character. The seasons come and go in the way God has planned, and the right type of work needs to be done at the right season, otherwise precious time is lost. The seasons don't give extra time for those who are late or slow. Learn to work fast. Sometimes we are just too slow to respond to certain things. One writer observed that there is always a gap or space between stimulus and response, and that the key to both our growth and success or prosperity is how we use that space or gap.[12] Once a season is missed, it's a great loss for the entire year. This is again the reason that lazy people are called upon to go and learn from the industrious ants. They collect their food while the weather allows them to engage the outside world without endangering themselves.

"Go to the ant, you sluggard; consider its ways and be wise! It has no commander, no overseer or ruler, yet it stores its provisions in summer and gathers its food at harvest" (Proverbs 6:6–8).

We must understand that there are times when we cannot be productive, so the thing to do is to work and prepare for such times when we can work, as the situation allows. This is precisely what Joseph did.

Chapter Four

CHILDHOOD EXPERIENCES OF SOWING AND HARVEST

The terms sowing, reaping and harvesting are practical agricultural terms that my experiences as a child have helped me understand. I saw that in order to obtain a good harvest it was necessary to work hard, and also act wisely.

In 1972, I was a very active and energetic eight-year-old boy, and up to a lot of mischief. My father once caught me baptising his chickens in a bucket of water. You see, I had been to church that morning and for the first time had experienced a baptismal service. I therefore thought it would be a good idea to baptise a few chickens so that they would make heaven too.

My father was furious. Drowning the chickens in the waters of baptism would have resulted in a great loss to the family, as we were dependent on the sale of their eggs to supplement my father's meagre income. That was the only time my dad ever smacked me.

I was indeed a challenge and this proved difficult for my mother. To save me from myself and the influence of some of the township boys, it was decided that I was not to remain in the township over school holidays but was to be sent to the village to be tamed by the tough experiences of herding cattle, tilling the land and spending the whole day in the bush with animals. So when the holidays came, I was sent to stay with my uncle Richard. It was in this period that I experienced first hand the life of a peasant farmer – working in the fields, sowing, reaping and harvesting.

I spent all of my school holidays over a five-year period on that farm, and although this was designed to break me and tame me, it turned out to be one of the greatest blessings in my life. I learned a lot of things in my time there, about hunting, fishing, looking after various animals, harvesting honey and milking cows. But the most important thing I learned was the patience of the farmer and all the activities involved before one could partake of the harvest.

Our life in the village was dependent on the seasons. The winter months ran from May to July. This was a time of preparation for the ploughing and sowing season, and involved, amongst other things, breaking in the juvenile oxen and preparing them for their work during the ploughing season. Around the month of August, we would dig out the manure from the cattle kraal (their enclosure) and spread it in the fields to enrich the soil with its much-needed nutrients. We would then dig over the soil with the oxen and plough to blend the manure into the soil. There would then be a short reprieve until the end of October when the real ploughing would begin. This involved waking up at around five in the morning and tilling the land, until around twelve noon when we got a quick meal before we took the goats and sheep to graze in the bush. There was no idle time!

As the rains fell, the crops grew, but so did the weeds. This heralded the beginning of the season of weeding. These weeds had to be removed because, if left, they would compete for nutrients with the crops and outgrow them, so we had to remove them and that was not easy. Our work did not end here though, because as the crop grew ready for consumption and the harvest loomed, it became a prime target for baboons and wild pigs, so it had to be guarded. If it wasn't, we risked losing all we had worked for all year long.

Harvest time involved a lot of work, but it was my best season as we were allowed to roast, cook and eat some of the maize. The condition was that we eat from the edges of the field where the crop was usually small. The middle of the field yielded a big crop and this is where the seeds for the coming season, and those used to produce corn flour, would be taken from.

This experience helped me understand why poor people in the Old Testament times were allowed to harvest around the edge of the field. This was simply because the crop was much smaller there but could still serve the purpose of feeding those in need without causing any significant loss to the master.

As time went on, the crop would dry up and this was the time to harvest. The crop would be cut down and placed in a heap where the maize would be removed from the stocks and placed in a well-aerated container for it to dry. After drying, it would then be removed from the cobs and placed in a storehouse, ready to be ground for food or set aside for the following season's seed.

My uncle was a wise man, and he knew that to have a good crop, you needed good seed. His seed had to be good quality, so we kept the seeds from the big crop, and he would even add some chemicals to it to ensure the seed was not destroyed by insects as it lay waiting to be planted when the season for sowing came along.

I noticed that other farmers who were desperate sold most of their big crop for money to pay their children's school fees and other family needs, and used the smaller crop for sowing. This resulted in smaller yields in the following years. It was quite simple: whatever a man sows, that he shall also reap – a biblical principle I saw practically demonstrated on that farm.

Now, with food available after the hard work, we were in a position to give and help those who had not obtained much from their labour, either due to a poor harvest or destruction of the crops by animals. There was a communal spirit of support in the village whereby people shared what they had, giving to those who had lost. This was not done to gain greater harvests but to ensure nobody lacked. You see, our seed was intact, hidden away, and ready to be used and sown in the next season, so I never viewed the bags we gave away as seed for our future harvest. We gave because we had something to give. We had something to give because we worked hard.

Many people refer to the parable of the sower in Mark chapter 4 when the teaching of giving comes up. Countless times, we have been taught to sow the seed of our finances on good ground so that we can reap a harvest, and the harvest that is talked of is many times equated to a 100 fold. However, my time on the farm helped me realise a very interesting point. I noticed that whist Uncle Richard took the pains to select and preserve the good seed for sowing, and we planted those seeds on good, fertile land, when it came to the harvest, not all of those seeds yielded what we would regard as 100 fold – some seeds produced full cobs of maize, whilst some produced cobs with empty rows, or sometimes cobs with no maize on them! This, I now realise is in line with Jesus' teaching, as *verse 8* of *Mark 4* states: *"And other fell on good ground, and did yield fruit that sprang up and increased; and brought forth, some thirty, and some sixty, and some a hundred." (KJV)* The end of this verse is often left out, but it is very important as it clearly tells us that not all seed that falls on good ground yields 100 fold. This thus suggests that any teaching that claims that seed planted in good ground translates to a hundred fold increase is flawed.

51

As we can clearly see, the seed that falls on good ground varies in the degrees of yield, however, in my days on the farm, I never noticed Uncle Richard worry or get frustrated about this, because the low yield was only a small amount, and we had planted many seeds, so the harvest overall was always good. It is for this very reason that we are not to sow sparingly. If we are to use the analogy of the seed as being the abilities and resources God has given us, then, we are to put them to use and apply them in various ways, as our yield – the end result of our sowing, will vary. This is a practical economic principle in the bible to help us in our day-to-day lives. It is the same as not putting all your eggs in one basket. Even though the basket is new and strong, it may be stolen, you may drop it, or you may fall and lose all the eggs.

The bottom line was, each seed yielded a different amount of crop. However, this did not matter because the more seeds we sowed, the greater our harvest was. This is the same principle we should be applying now – we should simply work harder, and at times, smarter to make sure we prosper.

The book of Genesis tells us that God gave Adam work to do after He put him in the Garden, and that has been the way of man's livelihood ever since. Man has had to work hard to obtain wealth or treasure and possessions. This is what the Bible says and God has not changed it.

After the Lord destroyed the earth by the flood, God did not want to see destruction of that magnitude again. He established an order that would remain throughout Noah's life up to the present day. In *Genesis 8:22* He says: *"As long as the earth endures, seedtime and harvest, cold and heat, summer and winter, day and night will never cease."* We still see these seasons today, because God established them.

Chapter Five

UNDERSTANDING HARVEST IN THE OLD TESTAMENT

Genesis 26 tells the story of Isaac, who at that time was living in a land experiencing a famine. A famine is a food shortage so severe that it causes starvation. But there wasn't scarcity of food because people were not sowing. They were! There was scarcity because one of the systems God had originally put in place, the rain, was not falling. It was a time of drought. People could not change the situation; only God could.

The natural response was to move to regions that had good conditions and plenty of food. However, God instructed Isaac not to move, but to stay and sow, and promised to bless him *(Genesis 26:3)*. In bringing about this promised blessing, it is interesting to note that Isaac still had to work. He did not sit back, expecting a mighty harvest to happen miraculously because God had promised to bless him. God didn't do anything to make his life easier by suddenly growing food for him overnight. No, seed time and harvest time still had to take place; the process had to be observed. God stayed true to His own words in Genesis chapter 3: *"Cursed is the ground because of you; through painful toil you will eat of it all the days of your life" (verse 17).*

Genesis 26:12 reads: *"Isaac planted crops in that land and the same year reaped a hundredfold, because the Lord blessed him."* Isaac toiled, worked the cursed earth, broke it up and made conditions conducive for the crops to grow. He reaped in the same year because of the principle of seed time and harvest time, and God blessed his obedience and diligence.

There is an important lesson here that is sadly lacking in many Christian teachings today. You see, even with promised prosperity from God, we have a very significant part to play in the promise being fulfilled. God has His part, and we have ours. We miss out because the key to reaping a good harvest is the work we put in: *"Whoever sows sparingly will also reap sparingly, and whoever sows generously will also reap generously" (2 Corinthians 9:6).* This sowing referred to practical sowing, which meant work. This verse is actually admonishing us against laziness, not against giving too little. It was about a practical principle.

God spoke, Isaac mobilised all his workforce, cleared vast expanses of land, and no doubt got up at dawn for a number of weeks to till the land. I don't believe he did it for just an hour a day. I believe he worked for at least eight hours each day, just as we do. Really? Yes. Judging by the size of the harvest the Bible tells us he reaped, Isaac was definitely not a lazy man. The miracle was taking place but Isaac worked to make sure his part was done. Angels were not sent to do the work for him. After the sowing came the task of chasing away the birds to protect the seed as it lay in the ground. When the crop began to grow, weeding had to be done, and when it was ready, the harvesting had to be done. As the crop was harvested, the barns had to be built to store the harvest, and so on. All this called for a lot of physical work.

This is how the Old Testament people understood harvest and blessing or sowing and reaping. It was never an instant action, neither was it a sudden miracle. It was a process that required diligence, with a number of stages that needed a lot of planning and preparation.

Proverbs 10:5 states that *"he who gathers crops in summer is a wise son, but he who sleeps during harvest is a disgraceful son"*. This verse again teaches against laziness. There are many threats to the harvest if it is not collected on time. It could be destroyed by rain, birds and other animals, and so carelessness and laziness could easily lead to the loss of the entire crop. Harvest time was a time of work, and the work was to reap and collect what was sown into storage, ready for the next process, before it found its way into people's bellies.

The story of Joseph in *Genesis 42* is no different. We are told that his father, Jacob, sent his sons to go and buy food from Egypt because there was a famine in Canaan. Why did the nation of Egypt have plenty of food, yet the surrounding nations battled with starvation? It was God's blessing.

Does that mean God just filled their barns and blessed them? Not at all! There was a lot of hard work on the part of the Egyptians as a whole under the leadership of Joseph, a true man of God. That is how the patriarchs of the Bible understood prosperity. They put their back into it.

The harvest and the poor

According to the Law of Moses, the poor were due a share of the harvest, even though they had no access to fields and no means of production. The only condition was that they had to work for it, even though the field was not theirs. There was no room for laziness and idleness.

In *Leviticus 19:9-10* we read: *"When you reap the harvest of your land, do not reap to the very edges of your field or gather the gleanings of your harvest. Do not go over your vineyard a second time or pick up the grapes that have fallen. Leave them for the poor and the alien. I am the Lord your God."*

The corners of the fields had to be left for the poor and the foreigners, who had to go and work in order for them to have food. That was part of the harvest for the poor. The popular Bible story that illustrates this is the romance of Ruth the Moabite and Boaz. You can read the account in Ruth chapter 2.

Ruth was to work and glean for her upkeep just like any other stranger and foreigner in Israel at that time. But in Ruth's case, there was the addition of a miracle. Because of the favour of God upon her life, Boaz was interested in her and he told his men to help her. This could be classified as a miracle in modern day terms. Sometimes, God does intervene in our lives to help us, but it would be absurd to expect Him to do it all the time – yet some in the Church today expect exactly that. But to do so is to mistake a practice for a principle. We must differentiate between principles and practices and guard against making doctrines out of practices.

Principles, as one notable author observed, are like lighthouses. They are natural laws that cannot be broken and they surface within our lifestyles throughout all generations. The degree to which people recognise and embrace them moves them toward either survival and stability or disintegration and destruction. Principles are therefore fundamental in that they form guidelines for human conduct in any given situation, and they have been proven to be enduring, having permanent value.

A practice, on the other hand, refers to a specific action at a particular time. This does not transcend generations and it is not a fundamental guide for daily living. A practice that works in one circumstance will not necessarily work in another similar situation. This is precisely why we must make a distinction between practices and principles.

While practices are generally situational and tend to be specific, principles on the other hand are deep, fundamental truths that have universal application and apply to prosperity, family life, business and relationships of any kind.

Giving, offerings and sacrifices

When it comes to giving, a lot of Pentecostal preachers teach that we give in order to meet a need that we have. The gift therefore, they claim, becomes a seed that will grow in the hands of God and turn into a harvest. But natural seeds do not grow in the hands of God. They grow in the soil. How then can our giving grow in the hands of God? We must give something to God to work with, they say. But this idea reduces God to our level, because God does not need anything to do anything. He created the world from nothing, with nothing. His Word is very clear on this. God does not think like us. He does things differently to us: *"For my thoughts are not your thoughts, neither are your ways my ways,' declares the Lord" (Isaiah 55:8)*. If He decides to do something, He has no need of our help – though sometimes He wishes to involve us. We are misinterpreting His Word if we think we need to give something to God for Him to be able to work in our lives.

Some also claim that we can determine what we want back from what we give, and so there is an expectation to get back whenever we give. In this view, giving ceases to be an act of worship, because God is no longer the focal point of the giving process. Instead, the giver who is expecting from God becomes the focal point. When God is not the centre and focus, something is clearly wrong. A study of the Old Testament does not support this change of focus.

Therefore giving is not about making us wealthy; we do not give in order to prosper.

Why do we give?

The first instance of giving that appears in the Bible is an offering in Genesis 4, where Cain kills his brother, Abel, because he was jealous that Abel's offering was better received than his own. There is no mention here of an expectation to receive anything back, nor of any motivation for giving other than worship and thankfulness.

Cain and Abel were conscious of God and presumably they did what they were taught or had seen their parents do. They did not conjure up the idea of giving to God in order to get something back. We must therefore give with a consciousness of God and gratitude, with a desire to help or to do good.

Mark A. Snoeberger, a seminary professor at Detroit Baptist Seminary contends that, as far as Cain and Abel were concerned their offering was an act of respect, thanksgiving, homage and friendship, and did not imply any obligation at all.[1] People must not be obligated to give.

Some ministers claim that human beings give to God in order for Him to meet their needs. This cannot be further from the truth, because when you look at the account of Cain and Abel, you see that their needs were already met by God even before they gave their offerings. It is only because they had something that they were able to give. Why then was Cain's gift rejected and not multiplied after its kind, as the popular preaching goes, because after all, he did 'sow his seed' by placing it in the offering? The only reasonable explanation for the refusal of Cain's offering points to the real reason and purpose of giving, which is faith and obedience, which in my view he did not have. We must give out of a sense of gratitude, reverence and obedience to God's commands and promptings.

There is no evidence that the early Jews' motivation for giving was in order to receive, nor was it their need that spurred them to give. In the life of Moses, giving was not man's idea, neither was it a way of sowing in order to reap. It was a command and a directive from God.

God provided for the Children of Israel as they left Egypt, and during their wanderings in the desert that followed, they received manna and all their food supply without even planting a garden or sowing in a field. This is what Jesus referred to in *Luke 12:24 (NLT)*: *"Look at the ravens. They don't plant or harvest or store food in barns, for God feeds them. And you are far more valuable to him than any birds!"* They had all they needed and gave nothing to God, as far as we know, until an instruction from the mountain more than three months after they had left Egypt. *Exodus 20:22-24* states: *"Then the Lord said to Moses, tell the Israelites this: 'You have seen for yourselves that I have spoken to you from heaven... Make an altar of earth for me and sacrifice on it your burnt offerings and fellowship offerings, your sheep and goats and your cattle.'"*

In the next two chapters, the instruction is further expounded: *"Celebrate the Feast of Unleavened Bread; for seven days eat bread made without yeast, as I commanded you... No-one is to appear before me empty-handed" (Exodus 23:15).* This was a command direct from God; it was ordained by Him. Therefore, to attach any condition to your giving, as some people preach today, is simply ludicrous. It is tantamount to rebellion; it is gross disobedience.

It is evident from these accounts that the offering and giving as a whole was God's idea and He required it from His people whether they had needs or not. Giving was an act of obedience that translated into worship. This is also seen in the life of Abraham, when he was commended for his obedience after demonstrating his willingness to sacrifice Isaac.

Abraham and Isaac – obedience

Abraham and Isaac have a similar story in *Genesis 22*. This is one of the first instances where God is specific about what He requires as an offering *(verse 2)*. Unlike some teachers today who claim that people give as a seed for what they are hoping to receive back from God, Abraham was prepared to give Isaac without expecting anything in return. If anybody had a reason to expect anything from God in return for his obedience, it was Abraham, by virtue of the promise made by God Himself. But Abraham did not ask for more children to replace Isaac, because the Lord had already told him that the increase of his seed would be a great nation through Isaac. Abraham must have wondered how on earth that could happen if he sacrificed Isaac, but he trusted God. *Hebrews 11:19* tells us that Abraham believed that God could resurrect Isaac. But whatever went through his mind, he was obedient.

So Abraham went on to nearly sacrifice Isaac, not because he wanted something from God, but because of his reverence and fear of God and obedience to His instruction. The angel's response to Abraham was: *"Do not lay a hand on the boy... Do not do anything to him. Now I know that you fear God, because you have not withheld from me your son, your only son" (verse 12)*. We must therefore fear God and do whatever He says, if we are to experience His full blessing.

The JF Bible Commentary says: "God did tempt Abraham – not to incite him to sin but to try, to prove, and to give occasion for the development of his faith... ready at a moment's warning for God's service."[2] This has everything to do with obedience! In Hebrew, to tempt, and to try, or to prove, is expressed by the same word, and that encompasses obedience.

Every trial is indeed a temptation and tends to show the character of the heart, whether holy or unholy. But God proved Abraham's heart was true to Him. Unlike some preachers, who would have seen this case as seed faith, and therefore considered Isaac a seed, God, the Angel and Abraham viewed it as obedience.

Kahlil Gibran, a Lebanese poet once wrote: "You give little when you give of your possessions. It is when you give of yourself that you truly give."[3] Abraham's attitude was similar when he offered Isaac. He was not thinking about himself and what he would get, as he was rich already. He was obeying a God who gave him that son in the first place.

Abraham believed that God knew what He was doing and therefore gave himself to God.

Noah and thankfulness

The story of Noah depicted in *Genesis 8* is another key in helping us understand the essence of giving as God intended. The King James Bible Commentary explains it very eloquently:

"One might think that having spent a year at sea, Noah's initial act upon stepping on dry ground would be to bend down and kiss the ground. But Noah was a man who walked with God *(Genesis 6:9)*, and now more than ever he recognised that salvation is of the Lord. Thus, *'Noah builded an altar unto the Lord'... Sacrifice offered by a righteous man in faith is always acceptable unto the Lord."*[4]

Now, God's response to this gift was not a multiplication of a hundred, or sixty or thirty-fold of the same kind of animals Noah had given, but rather, God was moved by Noah's action and appreciated his gratitude to the point of making a promise never to destroy the earth again. That was Noah's reward, and it was a good one that still stands today. The commentary reads:

"Therefore the Lord said in his heart, 'I will not again curse the ground any more for man's sake.' This determination did not arise as a result of the purity of man's heart. He was determining in himself never again to destroy the ground by a universal flood."[5]

Noah was not in any way giving to receive a multiplication of all he gave, neither did he determine what he wanted for his harvest. There was no good and bad soil because his heart was directed to God, who has no bad aspect in Him. He had no idea how God would respond and there was no expectation whatsoever. This offering was willingly directed to God, burnt up so that no man could interfere with it.

Matthew Henry, an English Commentator on the Bible in the 1700's has this to say about this passage: "Noah's thankful acknowledgment of God's favour to him, in completing the mercy of his deliverance, v. 20… He built an altar. Hitherto he had done nothing without particular instructions and commands from God. He had a particular call into the ark, and another out of it; but, altars and sacrifices being already of divine institution for religious worship, he did not stay for a particular command thus to express his thankfulness."[6]

Noah was alone when he came out of the ark, apart from his family. There was no man of God or financial mentor to goad him to give. He gave out of a thankful heart, with no expectations or conditions. God rewarded that, and today we are beneficiaries of that reward.

Jacob and his tithe

Looking closely at the story of Jacob depicted in *Genesis*, we see that in *chapter 28 verse 22*, Jacob promised to give a tithe to God. When analysed in context, it would seem that Jacob was not motivated to do this by faith and trust in

God. Instead, he appears to use his gifts to try to get God's protection because he is afraid.

This is supported by the fact that Jacob builds an altar and calls the place 'Bethel' in fear, not in faith (*see verses 18-22*)! He was not looking for prosperity through his giving as he was prosperous already. This wealth was acquired after a long period of working hard for his father-in-law, Laban.

Ernest Martin, the former chairperson of the Department of Theology at Ambassador College in Pasadena in 1973, observed that Jacob's conditions in the arrangement with God ('if' – *see verses 20-21*) mean it is doubtful that this form of gift could have been a seed planted for gain or further multiplication and a harvest.[7] He further questions why Jacob would have put a condition on something he believed would lead to his prosperity.

Snoeberger supports the view that the context favours the idea of fear rather than reverential awe and worship, and besides, Jacob shows a lack of faith in the explicit promises of God. Stuart Murray, a Bristol based renowned Christian author further argues that nowhere in Genesis is Jacob ever recorded as giving to God.[8] William R. Cunningham, the only gospel preacher to have a whole town named after him in the 1800's because of his influence in his community presents his understanding of Jacob's giving a bit different, but even so it clearly makes the point that in the Old Testament giving was viewed differently to how it is often thought of today.

Saul and Samuel

In *1 Samuel 9:7-8*, Saul and his servant discuss what gift to give to the prophet Samuel, before they ask him to tell them where some missing donkeys have gone. But they were giving because it was the tradition to bring a gift to a prophet, rather than trying to manipulate or bribe Samuel. They were merely being polite, following the common practice or protocol of the time. Samuel certainly did not demand a gift before he would tell them anything, and in the course of the story we see that he tells them what happened to the donkeys before they even get a chance to give him their gift.

So, this was a practice or custom of the time, and as I said earlier, practices are temporary – they are not principles that transcend the generations. When the queen of Sheba visits Solomon (*1 Kings 10*), she does exactly the same thing. Even though there would often be a reciprocation of some kind, the offering was not made in order to get something in return. It was just the tradition to give – as a sign of friendship, peace or admiration.

Chapter Six

SOWING OR GIVING?

I n the book 'Miracle Seed Faith', the writer tells a story
of how he needed a parish house and sowed a seed of
$50 – his entire weekly pay – and then challenged the
congregation to do the same.[1]

It is obvious that the writer had a conflict of interest here,
in that he knew quite well that he needed the house for
himself and that people would respond sympathetically to
his cause. But leaving that aside, he also erred in calling his
initial down payment of $50 his seed for his house. It was
simple obedience to the prompting of God, in a strategy
that would touch and move the congregation into giving in
his time of need – not sowing for a harvest as he would like
us to believe.

It is simply common sense to lead by example. If you desire
people to give to a particular cause, it's wise for you to give

first. If you want to be a leader, be prepared to part with what you want others to part with.

What makes this observation true is the next story the writer relates. He claims that on a busy morning he accidentally bumped his rich neighbour's car, and considered fleeing from the scene of the accident as he could not afford the repairs. But the Holy Spirit convicted him to repent and knock on his neighbour's door to confess and admit liability. Moved by his neighbour's honesty, the rich neighbour bought the writer a better car. Explaining this, the writer claims that the seed he planted for the house was now yielding even more fruit in the form of a new car. But this is not reaping after its kind any more. The theology has changed to suit the preacher, who is bound to benefit all the time, if this teaching is to be believed.

His story would make better sense if the seed he refers to was obedience, as this is the only common factor in both instances. This is where I think his misapprehension lies. In my opinion, the writer was rewarded for his obedience to the prompting of the Spirit, not seed faith! This tallies well with Abraham's story, in that Isaac was not the seed that was sown to bring about more sons. Instead, it was Abraham's obedience in trusting God by carrying out God's orders that resulted in his blessing, as *Hebrews 11:8* recounts.

Is it all about money?

The iLumina Encyclopedia has this to say about giving: "Giving appears on the surface to be sharing possessions, wealth, income, and the like. More important, giving is sharing itself. Giving is a most remarkable concept, originating in the heart of a giving God, a God who pours forth more blessings on His people than we can ever deserve or expect.

The gift of life, the gift of love, the gift of salvation, the gift of eternity in heaven – all of these are priceless. The possessions we have are generally a tangible result of what we have invested in time and energy and talent. But who we are, our character, is always a direct result of what we have invested of ourselves with God and others. And one of the great and unique promises of the Bible is that the more we give, the more we receive – not necessarily in material possessions, but in spiritual and eternal rewards.[2]

Looking at this definition, there is a suggestion right from the outset that sowing and reaping does not necessarily refer to our giving of offerings in monetary form only. The Encyclopaedia contends that even though the Bible says the more we give the more we receive, it does not just refer to material possessions but spiritual and eternal ones – implying that our rewards could also be received in the next world. The idea of teaching people to expect immediate and miraculous harvests is thus mistaken and misleading. The emphasis on money as a seed to be sown for a harvest is also misleading.

The teaching on sowing therefore must be balanced. What is it about money that makes some preachers seem to put it above souls and other actions of love? Why must God's blessing be linked with one's giving of money?

Some contend that money represents one's life, in that an awful lot of time and energy is spent accumulating it. But does this really compare with one's life?

Exodus 25 is an important chapter in the giving theory as it does not limit giving to money as the Encyclopaedia observed: *"Speak to the children of Israel that they bring me an offering. From everyone who gives it willingly... silver, bronze, scarlet thread, linen, oil, incense, stones... from twenty years old and above, shall give an offering to the Lord."*[3] We must quickly move away from placing money as the only means and way of giving if we don't want the world to accuse us of being lovers of money.

The Matthew Henry Commentary says: "It was not prescribed to them (the children of Israel) what or how much they must give, but it was left to their generosity, that they might show their good-will to the house of God and the offices thereof and might do it with a holy emulation."[4] On the same point the JFB Commentary has this to say: "Having declared allegiance to God as their sovereign, they were expected (by God) to contribute to His state as other subjects to their kings; and the 'offering' required of them was not to be imposed as a tax, but to come from their own liberal feelings."[5]

This is in sharp contrast to some preachers, who tell people to give specific amounts and then more, in multiples of 10, as an instruction from God. This has become a formula for some, and yet it is clear from the Scripture that God imposed no specific formula in what He did. The theology of giving in multiples is not only short of God's principles but an intelligently calculated practice to yield the maximum 'harvest' for those collecting the offerings.

There is a notable difference between the principle of giving and the practice of giving. We don't have to imitate the way someone gave and achieved success, otherwise it becomes presumption – a presumption that if we do exactly the same as someone else who received from God, then God must do the same for us. If God did not consider setting a cap on the Israelites' offering (after He had prospered them from the wealth of the Egyptians) through Moses' instruction, who the Bible calls the meekest man on earth, why then would the same God instruct another man of God to collect specific amounts and add on multiples of the same in order to reap a harvest?

Why would the same God do the same again in every state and country that the Gospel is preached, when He did it once for Israel? We must not repeat a certain practice just because it worked for certain people. Moses' first offering was clearly directed and accounted for, but today's prosperity teachers' accountability is often questionable.

My wife once attended a meeting where the minister claimed that he was sensing a strong anointing for financial breakthrough and the specific instruction to be followed was giving in multiples of seven. My wife only had a R20 note on her and was desperate to give as she needed a financial breakthrough. She looked around for R1 from the people around her in the congregation but could not get it. Although she had a desire to give, the instruction limited her and she came home broken and disappointed that she missed out on the blessing. Obviously, this was because she was misled by that man of God. How many more people are discouraged in church, a place that should be encouraging them just because they are R1 short? Was this a calculated move to maximise the offering? Is this how God works?

Sir Rodger Williams, the founder of the first Baptist church in America in 1639 had this to say on the subject of money: "He that serves God for money will serve the devil for better wages."[4] The Didache (one of the earliest writings of the early Church outside the Bible, attributed to the Apostles) clearly warned: "If any prophet, speaking in a trance, says, 'Give me money' (or anything else), don't listen to him."[6] This is the challenge to today's Pentecostal preachers, who distort the message of giving to ask for money from listeners.

"The rich are not to give more than a half shekel and the poor are not to give less when you make the offering" was the instruction to Moses in *Exodus 30:15*. Today the rich are pushed to give more in order to get more, when they already have more than enough! Is it really for them or for the preachers? There was no seed faith theology in the Exodus way of giving and no one was to reap anything from their giving. As far as God was concerned, all they possessed had come from Him in the first place. This was just a clear instruction and command that had to be obeyed.

The purpose of tithes

Today the message of tithes has been taken to extremes, with almost every television minister trying to get as many people tithing as possible, to keep their ministry going.

Some ministers get to the extent of monitoring if their leaders are paying their tithes. Some go as far as collecting the tithe when it was supposed to be brought in, according to Scripture: *"Bring all the tithes into the store house…" (Malachi 3:10a).* All this is in the spirit of raising as much money as possible. The reason for the tithe has long been forgotten.

Miles Bennett observed that there are three major passages related to the giving of tithes in the Law of Moses. These are *Deuteronomy 14:22-29, Leviticus 27:30-33* and *Numbers 18:21.* They are all related to the introduction of the priest's office and the tithes were given in order to sustain the Levites as their compensation for not being allowed to own land.[7] The gifts were commanded for a particular purpose, for sustaining the Levites, and note that they did not only take the form of money but of animals, land, seed and fruit. These other gifts, like land and fruit, could be redeemed with money by adding 20 per cent.

To this, Jacob Milgrom, a professor of Biblical studies adds that the tithe was God's idea to sustain His house (looking after the Levites), therefore making it mandatory![8] The Levites in turn were required to tithe to the other priests for their sustenance as well. This giving therefore was God designed and therefore should not have any strings and conditions attached by men. The people simply had the choice to obey the command or not. The blessings that followed those who willingly gave were handed out as God saw fit, not as givers demanded!

It is important to note that despite a change from the one-off giving that was used to build the tabernacle in the first offering Moses ever collected, the condition of *Exodus 25:2* (willingness, not coercion) still applies, even to us today. God never coerced His people to give and therefore the 'man of God' must take his example from God and not pressurise people to give to their TV channels and ministries.

The second type of tithe under the Mosaic Law, mentioned in *Deuteronomy 14:22*, was the festival tithe, and according to John MacAthur, author and editor of over one hundred and fifty christian books, this was considered a national 'potluck'.[9] The Children of Israel would bring a tithe of the produce of their fields or herds, and gather at a place determined by God and celebrate a particular feast, sharing and eating the tithe of food. If it was not practical to carry their crops or animals with them, they could sell these for money and then buy whatever they wanted to eat and drink. They were also specifically required to share with the Levites. It was all aimed at helping God's people enjoy a great feast. Giving to God is giving to those in need.

I once received an e-mail from a rabbi in Bristol (I contacted him in an effort to get an understanding from a Jewish perspective) who explained why such a requirement on people by God makes sense. This is what he had to say: "The misinterpretation of Scripture by Christians is nothing new to me. Misquoting Scripture with a false understanding is all too common. The fact is that Hebrew Scripture was written in a Middle Eastern milieu several thousand years ago. It is a complex multifaceted work with a variety of genres. Simplistic interpretations do not do justice. It needs prolonged study, serious consideration and generous, liberal minded, skilful teachers. Giving to others is simply practising hospitality."

The Scripture is a teaching encouraging us all to deal kindly with needy people. This is not in any thought of personal gain, though it does increase community spirit if society has more kind and generous people. That is what God commands; not because it is what God needs but because it is beneficial to human society.

From a Jewish perceptive, it is ludicrous to ever think of benefiting from giving. It is rather seen as obedience to a God who desires people to be like Him in order for them to live in harmony.

The third type of giving is explained in *Deuteronomy 14:28-29*. This tithe was for the poor, and it links well with the rabbi's understanding of giving in Jewish times. This was different from the other two in that it was given every three years and the purpose was to support the Levites, the foreigners, orphans and widows.

All these instances are directed and commanded by God in order to bring balance to society. Giving to those causes was considered giving to God. None of the people gave with an expectation to receive; neither did the Levites and the priests promise harvests and miraculous provision to people if they were obedient.

The prosperity of the people was not based on their giving but rather on the work of their hands and diligence. Peter Wade, professor of Anthropology and Christian author writes: "There are a number of considerations to the concept of giving. We should endeavour not to see it as a means of receiving what we want, but as an unconditional gift, otherwise the transaction is manipulative and the donation will not be a gift but more of a transaction, which is not the point. We should give because we want to and let nature take its course."[10]

Wade also contends that the timing of gifts to us is unlikely to match exactly our own gift. What, how and when we receive will be governed by everything going on in the world. We may even receive before we give. It is the wholehearted and unconditional attitude of giving that we should aim for, and let everything that is going to come our way do so, if and when it does. This was the heart of the famously selfless Mother Teresa. She always suggested that it was not how much we give but how much love we put into giving.

It is apparent from these instances that the attitude of giving in the Old Testament was nowhere linked to sowing and reaping as it is understood today. It was a mere act of obedience, worship and thankfulness for what God had already done, rather than what He was expected to do – as many Pentecostals are teaching today.

So that's the Old Testament. But what did Jesus teach about giving? We turn to that next.

Chapter Seven

JESUS' TEACHING ON GIVING

Today we are taught to give with an expectation to receive. Our money is a seed that will yield a harvest for us. But this is the opposite of what Jesus taught His disciples.

The popular giving chapter in *Luke 6* has a lot to teach us. *Verse 31* is key in understanding what Jesus is saying: *"Do to others as you would have them do to you."* This chapter is about living together as godly people. In other words, it is unreasonable for us to expect help from others if we do not do the same for other people. *Verse 38* then addresses our giving to one another:

"Give, and it will be given to you. A good measure, pressed down, shaken together and running over, will be poured into your lap. For with the measure you use, it will be measured to you."

This is not about God giving a harvest to us. It's about us sharing with one another, which is precisely what Paul teaches in Philippians and Acts. And the measure we give does not always relate to money, but rather, to day-to-day living out in the community. One evening I lent my car to my manager when his car broke down. It was a joy to assist him without expecting anything in return, although I did 'reap' half a tank of petrol when it came back!

To put it simply, when you live well with others and look after them in their time of need, one day, when you need their help, they too will give back to you and help you.

We very easily spiritualise this passage, but it is really a basic principle that even most unbelievers understand, follow and so live well with their neighbours. In other words, we give through good neighbourly practices – not just through the church offering basket.

In his article on giving generously, Jim Davis, an American gospel singer says: "God does not need what we have, he is more concerned with the attitude of our heart when we give. Freedom to give flows from the hand of the person whose mind views life from an eternal perspective... he is not expecting the poor to give him back... he trusts that the Lord will repay him in this life and/or in the life to come."[1]

So, in *Luke 6:38* Jesus meant that *"a good measure... will be poured into your lap"* by other people, not God, if you give generously to others. Therefore, telling people to give so that God will give the same measure "pressed down" is erroneous.

Jesus expounds this principle when He tells the Parable of the Shrewd Manager in *Luke 16:1-9 (NLT):*

"There was a certain rich man who had a manager handling his affairs. One day a report came that the manager was wasting his employer's money. So the employer called him in and said, 'What's this I hear about you? Get your report in order, because you are going to be fired.'

The manager thought to himself, 'Now what? My boss has fired me. I don't have the strength to dig ditches, and I'm too proud to beg. Ah, I know how to ensure that I'll have plenty of friends who will give me a home when I am fired.'

So he invited each person who owed money to his employer to come and discuss the situation. He asked the first one, 'How much do you owe him?' The man replied, 'I owe him 800 gallons of olive oil.' So the manager told him, 'Take the bill and quickly change it to 400 gallons.'

'And how much do you owe my employer?' he asked the next man. 'I owe him 1,000 bushels of wheat,' was the reply. 'Here,' the manager said, 'take the bill and change it to 800 bushels.'

The rich man had to admire the dishonest rascal for being so shrewd. And it is true that the children of this world are more shrewd in dealing with the world around them than are the children of the light. Here's the lesson: Use your worldly resources to benefit others and make friends. Then, when your earthly possessions are gone, they will welcome you to an eternal home."

This is a natural phenomenon. We once had a neighbour who never attended other people's funerals. She never visited anyone in hospital and was always at odds with most people in the community. When she fell ill, nobody assisted her until my mother intervened, only after rebuking and correcting her on her sick bed. She eventually changed and started to participate in community activities with the others.

The steward was aware of this truth about human nature and he was proactive about it. He did not spiritualise it. He came to his senses and acted on time and his master admired him for it – even though he'd been dishonest.

If you help people, most people don't forget who helped them, and when your need arises, as it says in *verse 9*, they will be much more likely to help you. This is what Jesus meant when He said that if you give it will come back to you, *"pressed down, shaken together and running over"*. This is Jesus' idea of giving to other people.

However, we must not give with an expectation to get anything back, but rather, give out of a heart of love and care, with no expectations. That is how our Lord operated.

Jesus' attitude and understanding on giving is clear in Scripture. In *Matthew 10:8* He says: *"Freely have you received, freely give."* In this case "freely" means without expectations and with gratitude, because you have received freely from God.

Whenever the crowds were hungry, Jesus would always tell His disciples to give them something to eat. He had numerous opportunities to ask them to 'sow a seed' but that was not the gospel He preached. Even in the case of the young boy with bread and two fish, which were miraculously multiplied, Jesus never mentioned sowing and reaping to the boy or the disciples.

Jesus' attitude on giving is best summed up by His words quoted in *Acts 20:35: "It is more blessed to give than to receive."* His focus is not so much on receiving, because in eternity we will receive far more than we can comprehend in this life. Concentrate rather on giving.

If we look at the story of the widow's mite, Jesus never addressed the widow directly; neither did He rebuke the stingy rich people. He did not promise the widow a return on her offering; He just mentioned His observation to the disciples. Here, the means of the giver and the motive are the measure of true generosity, and this is what God requires from us.

Mark 12:13–17 tells the story of the Pharisees attempting to test Jesus on giving. His response in *verse 17* was clear: "Give to Caesar what is Caesar's and to God what is God's." Jesus understood offering and giving from God's perspective. God does things differently to the world and true giving should be done in accordance with His rules – in this case, giving willingly! Does He not say it in *Isaiah 55:8: "For my thoughts are not your thoughts, neither are your ways my ways"*?

Matthew 19 gives an account of a conversation between Jesus and a rich young ruler. Jesus had a wonderful opportunity to receive an offering from the rich young man but instead He said to him: *"If you want to be perfect, go, sell your possessions and give to the poor, and you will have treasure in heaven. Then come, follow me"* (verse 21).

What Jesus was looking for was obedience in the heart of the giver. It would appear as if Jesus wanted the young man to be as obedient to His words and commands as he had been obedient to the Law from his youth *(Matthew 19:20)*.

Jesus did not say, "Give me your money and I will give it to the poor", but told the man to give it to those in need himself. It is important therefore to realise that giving does not have to be to a minister but to whoever has a need. This trend is maintained by the early Church in *Acts 4:34-35*. As far as Jesus is concerned, God lives in His people, and when you give to His people, you give to God. A lot of modern day preaching would like us to believe that our giving has to be directed at the preachers on God's behalf, but this is not the example shown by Jesus.

There is something terribly wrong when all of your giving is directed to one person to "use as the Lord leads them" when really, the Lord should be leading you to go and give to those in need yourself. I am not suggesting that we do not give to ministers or ministries; give! But when you do give, ask yourself why you are giving. Be led by the Spirit, not emotion, and be obedient to God in your giving. That way you are sure that what the Lord has given you goes into the right hands. Sometimes what is given is misused and wasted.

In a similar way, *Luke 19:1-10* tells the story of Zacchaeus. In *verse 8* he says: *"Look, Lord! Here and now I give half of my possessions to the poor, and if I have cheated anybody out of anything, I will pay back four times the amount."* Now, Jesus didn't ask him to direct this money to God through Himself, nor did He persuade him to give to the poor. Rather, Zacchaeus willingly gave up his ill-gotten wealth and restored it to those who it came from. He wasn't sowing a seed, expecting a harvest, because he had no needs at all – he had more than enough. His act of repentance brought salvation to his household *(Luke 19:9)*.

Riches and possessions must not consume us and divert us from the reason why Jesus came. *"Watch out! Be on your guard against all kinds of greed; a man's life does not consist in the abundance of his possessions,"* Jesus said *(Luke 12:15)*. After that He advises people to be rich towards God *(verse 21)*. How does one get rich towards God? Obviously this must be another form of riches, other than money, that the Bible teaches we should strive to possess. This heavenly wealth is the good works that the Apostle Paul is always exhorting his followers to be rich in.

In *Matthew chapter 6* Jesus teaches that God looks after birds that neither sow nor reap and lilies that grow without working, and then concludes with a question: *"If that is how God clothes the grass of the field, which is here today and tomorrow is thrown into the fire, will he not much more clothe you, O you of little faith?" (verse 30)*. The kingdom is not about money, riches and financial harvests but righteousness, peace and joy in the Holy Spirit.

87

Jesus and the tithe

Jesus never condemned tithing nor commanded that the Pharisees or the disciples begin or stop tithing. As far as He was concerned, tithing was good, but it was a lighter aspect of the law – much less important than justice, faith and mercy. The question He asked His disciples reflects this concern: *"However, when the Son of Man comes, will he find faith on the earth?" (Luke 18:8).*

In *Matthew 23:23* Jesus says: *"Woe to you, teachers of the law and Pharisees, you hypocrites! You give a tenth of your spices – mint, dill and cummin. But you have neglected the more important matters of the law – justice, mercy and faithfulness. You should have practised the latter, without neglecting the former."*

This does not mean Jesus was prohibiting tithing, in fact He says they should have practised it. He was merely condemning the wrong attitude and motives of those who were tithing and those collecting the tithes. The tithe was a small part of what was required of them, yet they gave it far more importance, neglecting other more salient commands. Jesus was resetting the balance. We must not tilt the scales again through our gospel of sowing and reaping.

In *Luke 18*, Jesus tells a parable about a tax collector. In the book 'Interpreting the Parables', Craig Blomberg rightly concludes that this parable's main point is not tithing or stewardship, and certainly not giving to obtain, but humility.[2] Jesus clearly states the message of the parable: *"For everyone who exalts himself will be humbled, and he who humbles himself will be exalted" (verse 14).*

Jesus never told people to tithe or not to tithe, neither did He promise them a harvest from their 'seed'. He does say, however, that giving is part of the law and it should be practised with the same attitude that was observed in the Old Testament. It must be remembered as well that the first Christians were Jews and that would have made them givers and tithers in the same way as the Old Testament Jews, who never gave in order to get more, but as a way of worship.

Jesus and miracles

Jesus performed numerous miracles, but interestingly He never created money nor encouraged people to sow money in order to obtain a harvest. In fact, the only time He performed a financial miracle was to pay for His taxes and those of Peter *(Matthew 17:27)*. That money came free from a fish, not an offering. God knows where the fish got it from, and the accuracy and probability of catching the right fish with the coin from vast waters is in itself a wonder! But it was a one-off. Jesus didn't live on financial miracles. Jesus knew precisely when to perform a miracle, but it was never a matter of routine. Today, almost every preacher is seeking to perform miracles every day of their lives and they are even advertising for them. Jesus never did that. Miracles were miracles indeed! A surprise!

The purpose of these miracles was for the Father to be glorified, so Jesus only performed miracles that would be a signpost to God. His miracles were so effective that we still talk about them today. He did not use His power for trivialities, but to make important points that would speak of God's compassion, provision, protection and salvation. His miracles were never for personal gain or to glorify Himself. He even told many of those He healed to thank God in private and keep quiet about it in public!

Today it seems that miracles, especially financial ones, are often sought not to give God the glory but to gratify man's appetite and greed. No wonder many Christian givers are disappointed; they have been conned! They have sown alleged financial seed after financial seed to reap this mighty harvest, but to no avail.

When hungry in the wilderness during a fast that lasted 40 days, Jesus was approached by the devil, who tempted Him to perform a miracle. The devil's aim was for the miracle not to glorify God but to serve the devil's purposes, and Jesus knew it. Sometimes certain challenges are just tests in order to develop our character, but many of us have been taught to seek a miracle to escape from an uncomfortable situation. Jesus did not do that. Paul understood this as well: *"I know what it is to be in need, and I know what it is to have plenty. I have learned the secret of being content in any and every situation, whether well fed or hungry, whether living in plenty or in want" (Philippians 4:12).* That's not to say that Paul wouldn't pray for God's provision for him, but nowhere does he speak of sowing so that he might reap a harvest to avoid being in need.

One of the devil's tests for the starving Jesus was: *"Tell these stones to become bread" (Matthew 4:3)*. This was a good opportunity for Jesus to show His power was far superior to the devil's by performing a miracle, and many of today's preachers would have jumped at the opportunity and tried to call on God. But Jesus did not do that. He was not in a macho miracle contest. The devil was no match for him. He sought to glorify God in every miracle that He did. His response was: *"Man does not live on bread alone, but on every word that comes from the mouth of God" (Matthew 4:4)*. That was Jesus' heart and the root of the sowing and reaping gospel, to obey what God commands us to do in any given situation. It is not about me, me, and me. We live not only by finances but by every word that comes from the mouth of God.

The real harvest

Jesus understood the principles of God and spoke parables that show people the importance of working. In *Matthew 9:37-38* He says to the disciples: *"The harvest is plentiful but the workers are few. Ask the Lord of the harvest, therefore, to send out workers into his harvest field."* We should be working to bring in the harvest of God, as this verse points out. But note that He says it's the Lord's harvest, not ours! Again, He is not talking about a money harvest, nor is He asking us to pray for a miracle, but the prayer must be a request for labourers who will sacrifice their agendas to help Jesus gather His harvest. Then, and only then will the rewards be given to the helpers.

Why pray for labourers, not a miracle? Jesus understood that with every harvest there must be work. Jesus always considered His ministry to be work. When responding to the Pharisees regarding working on the Sabbath, He told them: *"My Father is always at his work to this very day, and I, too, am working" (John 5:17)*. The harvests that are not accompanied by work, as promised these days, are not a harvest but a misunderstanding of Scripture, at best. At worst, they are a deception, leading you to be ripped off without realising it!

When Jesus saw the crowds in the cities He visited, the Bible tells us in *Matthew 9* that *"he had compassion on them, because they were harassed and helpless, like sheep without a shepherd" (verse 36)*. Yet he never taught them to give to Him, the Great Shepherd, or to plant a seed in order for them to prosper.

What do you see in the people around you? I guess some prosperity ministers merely see a prospect for an offering, while others, out of genuine compassion, will mistakenly see them as poor people who could reap more if only they would give something.

Numerous stories from the Bible are used to promote the prosperity message. For example, the widow's offering at the Temple *(Luke 21:1-4)*. She gave all that she had. Yes, she did give all, but does the Bible say we must also give all each time a sermon about her is preached? Not at all! This is not the principle being taught by this story. The principle is generosity and sacrificial giving. Jesus was not talking to the general public in that story. He was telling His disciples about the lack of generosity the leaders and the rich were showing in their giving, because they could afford to give far more than the widow. He simply made an observation and communicated it to His disciples.

When the Spirit of God impresses on you to give all, then by all means do so. We must learn to obey the promptings of God daily. That is what being led by the Spirit is all about. But don't take the widow and two coins story as some sort of command that we should all give all we have, all the time. Nowhere does Jesus say that if we give all the money we have, we will get back loads more. The Bible does not even tell us whether the widow herself benefited from her giving in this life. But you can be sure God noted her generosity.

Two other popular stories told in support of the prosperity gospel are from *2 Kings 4*. First, in *verses 1-7*, Elisha the prophet helps a poor widow who is in debt, and whose creditors are threatening to take her sons into slavery. When she follows his instruction, the little oil she has multiplies. Her oil does not run out until it has filled all the empty containers in her village. She can then sell the oil to pay off her debts. Prosperity teachers take this to mean that if we give a little to God, He will multiply it back to us. Instead, what this story is really teaching us is that God cares about the poor and will supply all our needs if we ask Him, and if we are obedient.

In the second story, in *verses 8-37*, a Shunammite woman gives Elisha free food and accommodation. Later, out of gratitude for her help, he prophesies that she will have a son, because she is childless. And later still, he restores that son to life. Prosperity teachers say this is an example of a believer giving to the man of God first, before meeting our own needs, and that if we do the same we will receive miracles of provision like hers, in return. This is a gross distortion of the meaning of this story. It does not mean that we have to give to men of God first in order to have our needs met. The Bible does not say that. The woman was not putting Elisha before her own needs. *Verse 8* says she was *"a well-to-do woman" (NIV)* or a *"wealthy woman" (NLT)*, so although she was being generous, she could no doubt afford to take care of her own needs at the same time.

We must not operate on presumption or imitated faith. There is nothing like organic, spontaneous, personal faith! God has no formula, He works differently every time, and the key is to trust Him whenever He speaks to us and respond accordingly. The Shunammite woman never expected anything from the man of God; she merely gave.

I had a discussion with a rabbi about the same passage. He informed me that Hebrews are always taught to be kind to strangers and this woman was merely practising what Jews do all the time. Copying what she did because it worked for her and then expecting to have a great reward is not faith, but rather an assumption that God has provided a formula for abundance. This is not true. It is good to teach the faithfulness of God and how the true servants of God operate, but it would be folly to think it will work for us the way it did for them. Our circumstances are totally different.

Now let's look at what the Apostle Paul taught about giving.

Chapter Eight

PAUL AND
THE HARVEST

A good place to start when you begin to think about attitudes to giving and finances in the New Testament is the life and teachings of the apostle Paul. He tells us in *Philippians 4:9* to follow his example: *"Whatever you have learned or received or heard from me, or seen in me – put it into practice. And the God of peace will be with you."*

Propagators of the 'sowing and reaping' message quote a lot of Scripture written by Paul. However, these Scriptures have been misunderstood or quoted out of context to fulfil an underlying agenda, while Paul used the sowing and reaping analogy to put a different point across.

Paul clearly lays out his heart and understanding of this doctrine when instructing the leaders of the church in Ephesus before his departure, in Acts 20. The first point was to call them to remembrance of his heart and behaviour and way of life, in *verse 18*:

"You know how I lived the whole time I was with you, from the first day I came into the province of Asia."

Paul's practice interprets his statements. So, if we are to interpret his statements, and so apply the Bible correctly, we must also examine his lifestyle. In *Acts 20:26* he testifies that he was innocent of the blood of all men. In other words he did not abuse, rob or take advantage of anyone in the way he proclaimed the Gospel. As a Jew, Paul understood seed time and harvest time in the sense of the Old Testament. This included work for day-to-day living. Paul performed a lot of miracles – people were healed, and at one point he even raised a young man called Eutychus from the dead. Yet there is no mention in Scripture of Paul asking for a miracle of provision for his food. Although he was a minister of the Gospel, he had a job. *Acts 18:3* clearly tells us that he was a tent maker: *"… and because he was a tentmaker as they were, he stayed and worked with them."*

Acts 20:33–35 reads: *"I have not coveted anyone's silver or gold or clothing. You yourselves know that these hands of mine have supplied my own needs and the needs of my companions. In everything I did, I showed you that by this kind of hard work we must help the weak, remembering the words the Lord Jesus himself said: 'It is more blessed to give than to receive.'"*

Paul undoubtedly reminds the leaders that he never shunned work as a means of provision for himself. Although he says that his God will supply the Philippians' needs according to His riches in glory by Christ Jesus, he is practical in telling the leaders that his needs were supplied by his hands. Is this a conflict? Certainly not! He understood that even though he was regarded as one of the greatest apostles, the law of sowing and reaping still applied to him in a very practical way – not in the way it is being taught today. Paul understood that work is what brings about food and sustenance, not miracles. Miracles are God's way of showing Himself as supreme for a specific reason and purpose, whenever He chooses to. There will be an occasional miraculous provision here and there, but that is not the norm as there are principles God has already put in place for sustenance and survival.

Rather than just praying for the weak and expecting God to intervene, Paul understood that the weak were to be supported by the labour of those who were strong – and this is precisely what he did. He remained within the boundaries of Scripture, even as James said: *"What good is it, my brothers, if a man claims to have faith but has no deeds? Can such faith save him? Suppose a brother or sister is without clothes and daily food. If one of you says to him, 'Go, I wish you well; keep warm and well fed,' but does nothing about his physical needs, what good is it?" (James 2:14-16).* James calls this dead, misdirected or useless faith.

Paul tells us that he was showing practical faith to the leaders. He experienced the success and victories he did because he deliberately adopted the lifestyle of his Saviour. It is sad to say that the lives of many ministers today are not like Paul's life at all. We do not do the things he did, although we are good at quoting him.

Paul also strongly elucidates this principle of how to provide for ourselves when writing to the Ephesians. The Ephesians were one of the churches the Lord commended in John's vision in the book of Revelation, and this was the commendation: *"I know your deeds, your hard work and your perseverance. I know that you cannot tolerate wicked men, that you have tested those who claim to be apostles but are not, and have found them false. You have persevered and have endured hardships for my name, and have not grown weary"* *(Revelation 2:2–3).*

How did they persevere? In *Ephesians 4:28*, Paul wrote to them about practical Christianity saying: *"He who has been stealing must steal no longer, but must work, doing something useful with his own hands, that he may have something to share with those in need."* The Ephesians complied. In the words of the great Welsh preacher and teacher Selwyn Hughes regarding training, Paul was literally training the leaders in the way they should go so that when they were on their own, they would not depart from it. This was the standard.

Working to survive

Paul worked with his own hands to provide for himself and those around him because he knew that it was a joy to give. It was a blessing, and it was in line with the character of God. In *Philippians 2:4* Paul writes: *"Each of you should look not only to your own interests, but also to the interests of others."*

He never spoke about a harvest or sowing a seed. He had the heart of Jesus Christ and wanted the same for the Ephesian leaders. He writes in *1 Thessalonians 2:9-10: "Surely you remember, brothers, our toil and hardship; we worked night and day in order not to be a burden to anyone while we preached the gospel of God to you. You are witnesses, and so is God, of how holy, righteous and blameless we were among you who believed."*

Since the fall of man, work and labour has become necessary for our basic survival. This was the consequence of Adam's disobedience. *Genesis 3:17-19* reads: *"To Adam he said, 'Because you listened to your wife and ate from the tree about which I commanded you, "You must not eat of it," cursed is the ground because of you; through painful toil you will eat of it all the days of your life. It will produce thorns and thistles for you, and you will eat the plants of the field. By the sweat of your brow you will eat your food until you return to the ground, since from it you were taken; for dust you are and to dust you will return."*

Sure, after the fall of man, Jesus came to save us, but not from working the ground! The Bible clearly says that God "vented" his anger against the ground, making it hard and tough, and then ordered the man to till it in order to survive, as his punishment. The Bible is clear that this will happen until man dies.

Paul understood this because he continued to work even though he was a missionary, and also encouraged his followers to do so. The people in Biblical times were hard workers because they understood that, 'Whatever a man sows, that shall he reap' was a statement based on the practical intricacies of working with one's hands. *Malachi 3:6* tells us that God never changes: *"I the Lord do not change."* Therefore, this principle still applies to us today.

Galatians 6:7-8 says: *"Do not be deceived: God cannot be mocked. A man reaps what he sows. The one who sows to please his sinful nature, from that nature will reap destruction; the one who sows to please the Spirit, from the Spirit will reap eternal life."* This is a spiritual allegory of the practical principle of sowing. It is saying that everything has a consequence. Repeatedly doing the wrong things will almost certainly have its repercussions because the wages of sin is death. So, if you sow into committing sin, your reward is death.

In verse nine of this same passage, Paul continues: *"Let us not become weary in doing good, for at the proper time we will reap a harvest if we do not give up."* In this case, you could say that 'good works' is the seed, and as you do good even when it is hard to do so, one day your goodness will result in change and that change will be the harvest or the result metaphorically.

Paul concludes in verse ten with the word 'therefore', meaning what follows is linked to what he has been saying before: *"Therefore, as we have opportunity, let us do good to all people, especially to those who belong to the family of believers."* In other words, I said what I said (in *verses 6-9*) in order that, as the opportunity arises, you will *"do good to all people."*

This is similar to what he says earlier in *Galatians 6:6*: *"Anyone who receives instruction in the word must share all good things with his instructor."* Here he is teaching people to be generous, and the seed again is good works.

Jesus says in *Revelation 22:12*: *"Behold, I am coming soon! My reward is with me, and I will give to everyone according to what he has done."* This is the future reward we should all be looking forward to, not the immediate harvest we are taught today.

It would seem from the emphasis in many Pentecostal movements today that everything must be achieved by a miracle. But miracles are provided by God as He sees fit – they do not come as an automatic 'slot machine' service of 'you put this type of prayer or faith in, and you get this miracle out'. If we lived in such a world of miracles on a daily basis, there would be no need for judgement and rewards.

Even though people sometimes can bless us with gifts, the real rewards of our work are coming with Jesus. This is what we should anticipate, and is the reason Paul encouraged people to good works. *Colossians 3:23-24* reads: *"Whatever you do, work at it with all your heart, as working for the Lord, not for men, since you know that you will receive an inheritance from the Lord as a reward. It is the Lord Christ you are serving."*

Please now take the time to read *chapter 4* of *1 Thessalonians*. It is clear to see that, in order not to lack in anything, the church (including the leaders) is commanded to work: *"Make it your ambition to lead a quiet life, to mind your own business*

and to work with your hands, just as we told you, so that your
daily life may win the respect of outsiders and so that you will not
be dependent on anybody" (verses 11–12).

This is not the teaching we hear nowadays. Could this be the reason why many people in the church are poor today? Believers willfully get into debt and expect God to get them out by a miracle, after sowing a financial seed. This is not scriptural.

Did Paul not say in *Philippians 4:19* that *"God will meet all your needs according to his glorious riches in Christ Jesus"*? Yes, he did, but what was the context in which he said that? It was in the context of gratitude for the sacrificial gifts he had received from the *Philippians (verse 18)* and prayerfully wishing that, in the same way, through people's generosity, God would supply their needs. It was a form of exhortation and encouragement; otherwise he would not have told the leaders at Ephesus that his own hands supplied his needs. It would have been contradictory!

Why do we ask for what we ask for? God is not mocked. He cannot be deceived into fulfilling requests because He already knows your heart. He already knows your needs, and He knows your wants too.

Paul is very clear on this matter. People had to work for their sustenance; if not, they were not to be given food. It is surprising that many people do not see this. In his conclusion of the second letter to the Thessalonians, in chapter three, he writes: *"Finally brothers... For you yourselves know how you ought to follow our example. We were not idle when we were with you, nor did we eat anyone's food without paying for it. On the contrary, we worked night and day, labouring and toiling so that we would not be a burden to any of you. We did this, not because we do not have the right to such help, but in order to make ourselves a model for you to follow. For even when we were with you, we gave you this rule: If a man will not work, he shall not eat. We hear that some among you are idle. They are not busy; they are busybodies. Such people we command and urge in the Lord Jesus Christ to settle down and earn the bread they eat"* *(verses 1-12).*

Nowhere in the pages of Scripture do we see the early Church being taught to give and expect a harvest or sow in accordance to the harvest they required and envisaged. The harvest was all catered for in the labour and work of one's hands, according to Paul. To consolidate this theology, Paul says numerous times to different audiences that they had to work night and day. Never in any of his teachings do we see him tell people to give in order to get. Neither did Jesus.

In our time, our desire to be rich, coupled with the 'sowing and reaping' message, has birthed a body of misguided believers who faithfully invest their money into ministries, expectant of a multiplication and a harvest of money one day. The Church has become to them almost like a high interest tax-free savings account with an indeterminate term time which they eagerly await to cash in on their return. I hope by now you can see that this really is not the way God intends.

The prosperity message has, however, resulted in the development of a wealthy group of pastors who are spending this money that is faithfully 'sown'. Many will claim that they are prosperous through their sowing and not through the offerings that they receive. Is this really so? If it is, then why is it only their sowing that yields great harvests for them? What about the rest of the congregation? Our desire and lust for financial rewards has created super rich ministers who reflect a totally opposite culture to the life of Jesus and the early disciples.

Chapter Nine

THE PASTOR AND THE OFFERING

I once took a trip to see a friend of mine who had recently moved to another city. At that moment in time he was staying in a pastor's house while trying to sort out his accommodation. On arrival at the pastor's house, we were met with a very unusual and tense atmosphere.

There was a lady clearing up plates from the previous day, and the dining table was set out for breakfast. Our friend came out to greet us, and promptly explained what was wrong. All this had begun on the previous day. The pastor had given an instruction which was not carried out properly, which had led to him being furious. The plates had therefore been left unwashed as everyone had fled the wrath of the man of God the night before. He was so angry in fact, that he did not want to attend the teaching service that evening.

He later changed his mind, pitching up an hour late for the service. He told them he was not preaching because he was too angry, closed the service after the offering, took the offering and went home to sleep. He was in fact still in bed on our arrival at the house.

I was speechless. If the pastor was so angry with the people, why take the money? Jesus taught that we should not even consider giving an offering if our hearts are not right. He told us to leave the gift at the altar and be reconciled before giving – let alone collecting – the offering. In *1 Timothy 6*, Paul challenges Timothy to flee from the love of money and pursue righteousness, godliness, faith, love, patience and meekness. All these traits were missing in the pastor that day. The only thing he pursued was money, and I can leave it to you to judge if such money was to be used for the work of God.

The next incident I wish to recall occurred quite a few years ago. I was in a different city from the one I have just mentioned, sitting in a meeting and listening to the pastor. As he spoke, he explained to us how the work of God needed finances for it to go forward.

He was so convincing and sounded very genuine and committed to furthering the Gospel. I was moved and felt that I needed to make a sacrifice. All I had was some money that was meant to go towards my rent, but I decided to sacrifice my 'Isaac' to the work of God. So, I put the money in an envelope and wrote on it my request to God as I sowed this seed.

I was keen to talk to the pastor, and had an opportunity to do so after the service. As we walked out of the church, two young girls flirtingly came over to him, and nagged and moaned about one thing or another. Their conduct suggested that they were very familiar with him. One of them mentioned that she was hungry, so this pastor took out an envelope from his pocket, opened it and gave them some money to go and buy some burgers at a nearby take-away.

I'm sure the girls were blessed by such a generous heart, but I was not! You see, that was the envelope with my 'Isaac' that I had sacrificed to further the Gospel. I knew it was mine because I spotted my writing on the envelope as he opened it. Worse still, that was not the only envelope he had. As you can imagine, I was disappointed and speechless. I learned a valuable lesson that day, as I realised that the man of God and his God are two different entities. I saw that the man of God is human, like me, and sometimes he can misuse God's money.

When I shared this incident with a few friends, we decided to write a letter to express our disappointment. In reply, we were told that once we gave the money it no longer belonged to us but to God. We had to pray so that He helps His servants to use the finances wisely. I don't know what you would like to call this? In my view it was daylight robbery, misappropriation of funds and a clear rip-off. We were told to sow, and I sowed, but I guess my seed fell on very rocky ground that day and the birds of the air (the two girls) came and picked it in my presence. What bold birds they were! That collection was not done for God. His name was just a tool that was used to get the money.

Although this incident occurred a while ago, it is a practice that still takes place today. That is why it is important for us as believers to be diligent when it comes to giving. Make sure you know what God these men and women are talking about; make no assumptions.

Another incident I recall involved yet another pastor. The church I was attending at that time needed some musical instruments. The total amount of money needed was calculated and pledges were taken, which covered the need. The pastor stood before the church and thanked us for our generosity, promising us that the instruments would be at church the following week.

To our surprise, there was nothing the following week but an excuse. The instruments arrived a week after that, which caused a lot of excitement, but surprisingly, they appeared old. We soon discovered why, when a visiting preacher turned up at our church to collect his musical instruments. As you can imagine, they had been borrowed to silence the church; some heated confrontations followed, and the pastor confessed that he had used the money collected for other urgent personal things and borrowed the instruments that we could now see. Fresh collections had to be made and we eventually bought the instruments.

As you can see, a lot is being done in God's name but without the God of that name. God has now become a tool to manipulate believers to give. I'm not saying all pastors do this; there are many honourable pastors out there and

I commend them for that, but the purpose of this book is to expose the anomalies in the Church today so as to bring awareness.

We must not be ignorant of what is going on around us. We must test every word that comes from the pulpit; that is how you discover the wolf in sheep's clothing. Otherwise, in your supposed diligent giving, you will never get a result or the blessing you seek. Learn to give the right way, with the right attitude to the right hands. The sad thing is that most people are oblivious to the daylight robbery that goes on in churches today. Some are aware of the deception but don't have the courage to stand up against it, as it involves God. They don't want to talk about it because they don't want to touch the anointed of the Lord. Really?! It is these supposed anointed of the Lord that are playing around with God's glory and His people, and they must be challenged.

I once sat in a leadership meeting where the pastor was chiding his fellow leaders and subordinates for failing to take good care of God's people. I thought that was a profound thing he had said, but what came after that quenched my excitement. "These people are our bread and butter," he concluded. I sat there stone faced with shock. Was this the reason the pastor wanted people in the church? To supply his daily bread?

Paul was different in his attitude: *"Keep watch over yourselves and all the flock of which the Holy Spirit has made you overseers. Be shepherds of the church of God, which he bought with his own blood" (Acts 20:28).* The reason Paul took good care of the flock was because he was constantly reminded that redeeming the Church cost Jesus His life. He shed His blood to buy us back. For this reason, Paul realised that he was a steward to the flock and therefore did not have any right to fleece them.

To many preachers, the term stewardship no longer seems relevant. Many ministers only allude to the word when they convince people to give and promise to be good stewards. How can they be good stewards to the money yet fail to be good stewards to the people who work tirelessly to give that money? It's like promising to take good care of the sheep's wool, meat and milk, yet we can't take care of the very sheep that produce those things. This is precisely what Paul was teaching the leaders of the Ephesian church in *Acts chapter 20*.

A steward is one who is entrusted with another's wealth or property and charged with the interest of managing it in the owner's best interest. The Bible requires us to have the mind of Christ, enabling us to have the same understanding as Him in our conduct and lifestyle, and so helping us to be good stewards of what He has entrusted into our care.

Peter issues a stark warning on stewardship: *"Be shepherds of God's flock that is under your care, serving as overseers – not because you must, but because you are willing, as God wants you to be; not greedy for money, but eager to serve; not lording it over those entrusted to you, but being examples to the flock"* (1 Peter 5:2-3). The reason is that, according to the next verse, the Chief Shepherd is coming, and when He comes, He wants an account of our labour.

The steward must understand accountability and the fact that every owner always wants an account of his business. Servants must understand the importance of faithfulness. The Scriptures teach that a servant should be found faithful (e.g. *Matthew 24:45-50; 25:14-30*). This faithfulness must be their priority until the owner returns and it does not matter how long the master takes, faithfulness is the life calling of the servant. In addition, wisdom and readiness for the master's return will instil a fear for the master with an understanding that when he stands before his master, he will be alone and the master cannot be deceived. *"Let each one examine his own work... For each one shall bear his own load. Do not be deceived, God is not mocked; for whatever a man sows, that he will also reap" (Galatians 6:4-7).*

First generation pastors

Timothy and Titus fall into a category I call 'first generation pastors'. There are obviously more leaders who fall into the same group under other apostles, but from the records of the New Testament, these two were very active with the apostle Paul and he even sent them to do some pastoral work as we understand it today. The two letters to these young pastors shed some light on how the Gospel message was passed down to them.

We need to look carefully at Paul's instructions to these two pastors because it will help us to know how modern day pastors should live, and how the Church should work.

111

Timothy

Paul gives a very clear warning in *1 Timothy 6*. In *verse 5*, he warns of *"men of corrupt mind, who have been robbed of the truth and who think that godliness is a means to financial gain."* He says: *"Flee from all this" (verse 11)*. Instead, he says, *"godliness with contentment is great gain" (verse 6)*. He continues: *"For we brought nothing into the world, and we can take nothing out of it. But if we have food and clothing, we will be content with that" (verses 7–8)*.

Paul was not saying we must be poor. He was merely instructing Timothy on the priorities as far as the Gospel is concerned. In *verses 11-12*, he says: *"But you, man of God, flee from all this, and pursue righteousness, godliness, faith, love, endurance and gentleness. Fight the good fight of the faith. Take hold of the eternal life to which you were called when you made your good confession in the presence of many witnesses."*

What is "all this"? The love of money is undoubtedly one of them: *"People who want to get rich fall into temptation and a trap and into many foolish and harmful desires that plunge men into ruin and destruction. For the love of money is a root of all kinds of evil. Some people, eager for money, have wandered from the faith and pierced themselves with many griefs"* *(1 Timothy 6:9-10)*.

Now, some may contend that they don't love money – they just want it – but there is a very thin dividing line between the two. In my opinion, if a preacher is making more altar calls for money than for repentance, that preacher has got a love of money.

Today there is a lot of focus on financial prosperity instead of the pursuit of righteousness, godliness, faith, love, endurance and gentleness, as advised by Paul.

Note that Paul also gives instructions to the rich in this passage. *Verses 17-19* read: *"Command those who are rich in this present world not to be arrogant nor to put their hope in wealth, which is so uncertain, but to put their hope in God, who richly provides us with everything for our enjoyment. Command them to do good, to be rich in good deeds, and to be generous and willing to share. In this way they will lay up treasure for themselves as a firm foundation for the coming age, so that they may take hold of the life that is truly life."*

The rich are told not to trust in their riches but in God, to do good and be willing to share. This is how the early Church worked, and no one lacked anything. Randy Alcorn sums it up very well when he says: *"God prospers me not to raise my standard of living but to raise my standard of giving."* We must continually realise that heaven, not earth, is our home and therefore our focus should be on heaven. By doing good, we lay up treasures in heaven.

Titus

Titus is taught precisely the same principles. He was sent to correct the things that needed correcting and ordain leaders so that the Christians in Crete didn't fall into the same trap.

113

The qualifications are clear in *Titus 1:5-9*.

An elder must:

1. be blameless
2. be the husband of one wife
3. have children who believe and are not wild and disobedient.

An overseer must:

1. be blameless
2. not be overbearing
3. not be quick-tempered
4. not be given to drunkenness
5. not be violent
6. not pursue dishonest gain
7. be hospitable
8. love what is good
9. be self-controlled
10. be upright
11. be holy
12. be disciplined
13. hold firmly to the trustworthy message
14. encourage others by sound doctrine and refute those who oppose it.

Most of our men of God are wanting when we look at these qualities. Paul wanted the baton of ministry to be passed on to faithful people who would not taint it. These were the conditions.

Today too many men of God fail to stick to one wife and still claim to love with the love of God. Something has gone wrong!

Titus was left in Crete to sort out the mess, as a lot must have gone wrong in order for these instructions to be needed, and in order for Paul to remind Titus of the Cretans' bad reputation *(verse 12)*. *Verse 11* says some people *"must be silenced, because they are ruining whole households by teaching things they ought not to teach – and that for the sake of dishonest gain."* Paul says they profess that they know God and yet deny Him by the very things they do *(verse 16)*.

God is a holy God and His servants must display that trait and spirit. This is how the early pastors were trained and this is how they were supposed to train those who came after them. Something has gone wrong since then! The good thing is that the records are there for those who want to go back and retrace the history in order to find those ancient paths again. The problem with many Christians is that they never check the Scriptures like the noble brothers in Berea *(Acts 17:11)*. They merely follow what they are told.

Reading back in history tends to show the flows and diversions from the common faith. Ian Murray regrettably notes the consequences of not studying history. He says: *"Not to know what has happened in the past is always to remain a child,"* and childish ignorance is no safe state for those who are called to fight against a superhuman power. We cannot do so until we begin to check the Word and correct all the wrong teaching going around about sowing and reaping today.

You don't need money to preach the Gospel

One of the most common excuses that people are given when they are asked to give is the fact that the preacher wants to preach the Gospel all over the world. So, they are in need of finances so that they can travel quickly to wherever the Lord may want to take them, or so that they can get on TV to reach the world. While all this sounds spiritual, it is not necessarily true. It may actually be that the preacher wants to be on TV because that's a way of raking in even more money from a wider audience.

The Gospel can be preached without money. What is needed, though, is the Holy Spirit, because preaching needs the backing of God through the power of the Holy Spirit.

When the Lord Jesus first sent His disciples out on preaching practice, he deliberately asked them not to take any money with them: *"After this the Lord appointed seventy-two others and sent them two by two... Do not take a purse or bag or sandals... Stay in that house, eating and drinking whatever they give you, for the worker deserves his wages. Do not move around from house to house... eat what is set before you" (Luke 10:1-8).*

They preached and people were healed and demons fled. *"The seventy-two returned with joy and said, 'Lord, even the demons submit to us in your name'" (verse 17).* Did they have money?

Apparently not! Did they preach the Word? Absolutely, and the testimony they left impacted many more. Later, Jesus asked them: *"When I sent you without purse, bag or sandals, did you lack anything? 'Nothing', they answered" (Luke 22:35).*

Someone may argue that the following verse states that Jesus then told them that they could take a purse for their future journeys, if they had one. That is true, but it does not nullify the fact that the Gospel was preached and signs and wonders were done on their first journey, without money. We cannot make a case or doctrine that money is a pre-requisite to preach the Gospel because it is clear that it is not.

The early Church was also not given a budget to preach the Gospel. This does not mean we must be foolish and fail to make adequate financial plans – absolutely not! But the disciples were told that they only needed the power of the Holy Spirit. This is the only pre-requisite. Jesus said: *"I am going to send you what my Father has promised; but stay in the city until you have been clothed with power from on high" (Luke 24:49).* This was the condition Jesus left.

Having walked and lived on earth, Jesus knew the importance of money to this world, but He also knew that His kingdom was not of this world and therefore not driven by money but by the Holy Spirit. The disciples were obedient and went to Jerusalem to pray, and waited until they were filled with that power from on high. *"When the Day of Pentecost had fully come, they were all with one accord in one place. And suddenly there came a sound from heaven, as of a rushing mighty wind, and it filled the whole house where they were sitting... And they were all filled with the Holy Spirit" (Acts 2:1-4, NKJV).*

Only after being filled with the Spirit did the apostles venture out to speak to the crowds, and, as recorded in *Acts 2:41, "about three thousand were added to their number that day."*

In *Acts 3*, a beggar asks Peter and John for some money. Peter responds that he doesn't have any. Was it an issue for them? Not at all! Did they feel less prosperous and powerful? It doesn't appear so, because when they offered him what they had instead, the entire city was electrified by what they saw. The Gospel had now been introduced God's way by the true witnesses. This was another kind of prosperity; the kind money cannot buy, and John says of it: *"Beloved, I pray that you may prosper in all things and be in health, just as your soul prospers" (3 John 1:2, NKJV).* So prosperity is more than money and wealth. The soul must prosper as well.

What seed then is sown for soul prosperity? Why don't we hear about it? Prosperity is a result of God's abundance and that cannot be denied! But the fact is that prosperity should not be the end in itself and must not be the emphasis of the Gospel. It must be the result of a quality of life, commitment, education and a life that is in line with God's Word. We must realise that the word 'prosper' in this verse means to help on the road or to succeed in reaching. In depth, it implies that divine prosperity is not a momentarily passing phenomenon, as the New Spirit Filled Bible puts it. It is an ongoing progressive state of success and well-being and it is intended for every area of your life, be it spiritual, material, emotional or physical. God therefore does not want us to emphasise any one area of prosperity, and the verse talks about prospering in all things! We must maintain a balance.

"Silver or gold I do not have, but what I have I give you." Peter and John had something to give even though it was not money. *"In the name of Jesus Christ of Nazareth, walk." The man did walk (Acts 3:1-10)*. I'm not sure what seed this would be classified as by the seed propagators but we are told that Peter gave healing. Did he give to receive? Absolutely not! Did he have a healing need himself? Not according to this account. Healing, to me, is another aspect of prosperity and it does not come by sowing money or giving an offering alone. It's much more than that.

It is apparent from *Acts 2* that the first ever preaching engagement in the history of the Church was empowered by the Holy Spirit, not by money. We cannot therefore claim that without money the Gospel cannot be preached. With the testimony of what God has done, the Gospel can go across the world without a single penny spent. That's not to say that we must avoid money, but money certainly does not warrant the attention it is given.

The fallacy that people must be pressured in order to sustain some TV ministry is not true. If we do what we are supposed to do as believers, there is not even a need for one person to be flying around the world because every believer will be preaching wherever they are, with the accompaniment of signs and wonders. The early disciples were so focused and disciplined that money was not an issue for them. People just gave willingly.

Faced with one of the most tempting circumstances of a man called Simon who wanted to buy what they had, Peter and John were resolute *(Acts 8:20)*: *"May your money perish with you, because you thought you could buy the gift of God with money!"* Money will never move God to do anything. It is our hearts. David talks about this in *Psalms 34:18* and *51:17*. Peter and John said to Simon: *"You have no part or share in this ministry, because your heart is not right before God."*

Today there are preachers who are even selling prosperity handkerchiefs! What a contrast with the early Church. When the leaders of the community arrested the first disciples and asked by what power they did what they did, the answer was very simple: *"Know this, you and all the people of Israel: It is by the name of Jesus Christ of Nazareth, whom you crucified but whom God raised from the dead, that this man stands before you healed"* *(Acts 4:10)*. That was the reason, not money!

In *Acts 2* we are told that 3,000 people joined the Church on the Day of Pentecost, after which *"the Lord added to their number daily those who were being saved"* *(verse 47)*. So by *Acts 4* the Church must have been a considerable size, yet *Acts 4:34-35* states that *"there were no needy persons among them"* because *"from time to time those who owned lands or houses sold them, brought the money from the sales and put it at the apostles' feet, and it was distributed to anyone as he had need."* This was the spirit of the early Church. None gave to get more; none sowed a seed in order to get more. They gave to bless those in need.

There was so much love and the people, walking in love, shared what they had. In addition, the leaders had integrity and so administered the gifts fairly. They used the money for what it was supposed to be used for. The apostles were not even concerned about money. They wanted to pray and fast and study the Word and preach. The logistics of daily distributing food to such a large church was left to the deacons, who were also full of the Holy Spirit. The apostles said: *"It would not be right for us to neglect the ministry of the word of God in order to wait on tables. Brothers, choose seven men from among you who are known to be full of the Spirit and wisdom. We will turn this responsibility over to them and will give our attention to prayer and the ministry of the word"* *(Acts 6:2-3).*

We don't see this heart in many preachers today. Pastors want to make every financial decision and want to control all the money. Many are preaching for the money. No wonder there is no evidence of the Holy Spirit. There is a lot of evidence of the presence of money but that cannot match what the Holy Spirit can do. The book of Acts shows us the true pattern of the Church and we need men of courage to call the Church back to the ancient paths.

King Solomon also demonstrated the way God's kingdom operates. While at Gibeon, the Lord visits him and asks him a question: *"What shall I give you?"* Solomon did not ask for a lot of money or wealth, even though that was ultimately also given to him. Instead, he asked for wisdom: *"So give your servant a discerning heart to govern your people and to distinguish between right and wrong" (1 Kings 3:9)*. The Lord was pleased with Solomon because he did not ask for *"long life or wealth for yourself" (verse 11)*. For that, God gave him wisdom as well as riches. Solomon's heart was for the welfare of the people in his kingdom, and in the same way pastors today should put the welfare of the people under their leadership before their own prosperity.

Elisha was no different when Elijah asked him what he wanted. He requested a double portion of the anointing that was upon Elijah's life, not riches.

Count the cost

Spreading the Gospel is all about the Holy Spirit, not money. He is the only one who will convict unbelievers of sin. It is He that gives to those who trust Him the boldness and openings to preach the Gospel, with or without money.

The Gospel should be an organised proclamation that is well managed, not one that is always appealing for funds. Today we hear that that the Church needs more money to be effective and to keep the Gospel being heard. While this might sound spiritual, the kingdom of heaven does not operate like that. One writer puts it well when he contends that not everything that requires more money is progress and not all progress means spending more money. Jesus demonstrates this very clearly throughout his life. The kingdom of God operates through faith and wisdom.

The great missionary Hudson Taylor put his finger right on the problem when he noted that when God's work is done God's way, it will never lack God's supply. If it is God's work, why must it lack then?

In *Deuteronomy 28:1-14*, God made a promise to those who follow and obey Him diligently. *Verse 12* says: *"The LORD will open the heavens, the storehouse of his bounty, to send rain on your land in season and to bless all the work of your hands. You will lend to many nations but will borrow from none."* The rain that was promised was to be at an appointed time (in its season), and the Lord promised to bless the work of their hands. God never promised to rain down a harvest without the people having to work for it. Israel had to do the work in order to get the money the Lord had promised. They needed to do their part, and He would do His. There was no miracle or short cut. This is the same God we serve today, and His principles have not changed.

What many fail to realise is that money is not a church's greatest asset. Rather, it is the Holy Spirit who is the asset. If a church or ministry is constantly in want of money, always begging, taking pledges, begging for donations, either it's not doing God's work or God's work is not being done God's way.

This is purely because if a church has the right God, the right leaders, the right people, and the right cause, then the finances will also be right. After all, didn't the Lord promise blessings if His voice is diligently obeyed?

The problem some churches have today appears to be lack of wisdom. Leaders engage in too many projects that end up being a burden to people, even though God has already put in place a respectable way of channelling finances into the local church for what He requires it to do. Our leaders must learn to prepare in advance for whatever task is at hand. Jesus calls this counting the cost. In *Luke 14:30* He says: *"Suppose one of you wants to build a tower. Will he not first sit down and estimate the cost to see if he has enough money to complete it? For if he lays the foundation and is not able to finish it, everyone who sees it will ridicule him, saying, 'This fellow began to build and was not able to finish.'"*

These are the words of the owner of the Church, Jesus Christ. His expectation is that believers must not make themselves a laughing stock in the work of the ministry. Planning and proper strategy is required to do God's work. God wants to lead us by His Holy Spirit. That is why He is our greatest asset. *"For as many as are led by the Spirit of God, they are the sons of God" (Romans 8:14)*. God's sons are organised, diligent, honest and wise, as Paul said to Timothy.

If we look back to the time of Moses and the building of the Tabernacle in *Exodus 36:1-7*, the offering was collected way before the building commenced. The work only began when everything was ready. Moses even stopped more money coming in because they had enough to complete the task. In fact, so much money was being given each morning that the craftsmen stopped working *"and said to Moses, 'The people are bringing more than enough for doing the work the LORD commanded to be done.'* Then Moses gave an order and they sent this word throughout the camp: *"No man or woman is to make anything else as an offering for the sanctuary. And so the people were restrained from bringing more, because what they already had was more than enough to do all the work."*

This is a practical example of doing God's work, God's way with the right people and the right leadership. This is how the Church should be working, in obedience to God as a form of worship. Today, some ministries are going as far as employing fundraisers, some of whom are not even born again, and then they receive a percentage of the donations for payment. This is a sure sign that God's work is not being done God's way.

Another good example can be seen in the life of King David. When he realised that he was not permitted to build the Temple because of his unclean record, he made preparations for Solomon by organising all the building materials in advance. He counted the cost. A lot of preachers today never sit down to count the cost. This results in a financial burden, and in an effort to raise the money needed, the preachers preach the message of sowing in order to receive and the greater the giving the greater the harvest.

Neglect of work for full-time ministry

There has been a huge diversion from the ways of our apostolic fathers and the Church is paying heavily for this departure from sound doctrine. Foolishness and lack of wisdom from unseasoned leadership has created the mess we are in.

In the 1980s there was a move of the Holy Spirit in many nations in Africa, but believers got caught up in wrong teaching. Most people were encouraged to leave their jobs and work for God full time, as God would provide for their needs. It was called a life of faith then, but was it really a life of faith? The principles of working with our hands for provision and survival were thrown out of the window, and preachers were suddenly called upon to get rid of their jobs and live by faith and God was to provide for them to prove Himself. Everything had to be a miracle.

Many people's lives were negatively affected as people suffered from lack. Very excited individuals abandoned work and came into full-time ministry. This resulted in a heavy burden on the churches as more people had to be supported from the church coffers. But the offerings were not enough because fewer people were working and therefore the flow of substantial offerings ceased. This resulted in some churches using pledges in order to meet their budgets. When this did not work, one church I knew resorted to collecting three offerings in one service, one before the preacher delivered the sermon, one soon after the sermon delivery and, finally, at the end of the service, people were asked to drop in whatever they had left on their way out.

All this was desperation, caused by lack of diligence and wisdom. When people finally realised the pastor's strategy of multiple offerings, they responded by breaking their offerings into smaller amounts to be seen to be responding, and consequently the funds never increased. This showed that God was not in it; it was riddled with scheming on both sides.

When this initial strategy failed, a gospel of sowing in order to reap surfaced. This worked for some time and still does in some areas. Whenever someone wanted a job, to pass exams or a promotion, they were required to put a seed towards that which they desired. If the sermon preached meant something to you, you had to put a seed; and a financial seed for that matter. All this was encouraged in the backdrop of meeting the needs of the church.

Nowadays people even go and give an offering during the preaching if they want certain things from the Word. Repentance is rarely stressed. At one point one church I know had to send one pastor to people's work places to collect the tithe because the church was under such pressure. They had the manpower but had pulled them out of work, and they suffered.

At one point the pastor would write a faith cheque and deposit it late afternoon on Saturday, and then pressure the people to give in order to meet the cheque before Monday morning. All this was done in God's name.

It is clear that God was not in this kind of work. Scripture warns us that the Church or God's people perish for lack of knowledge *(Hosea 4:6)*. We see from the life and teachings of Paul that he was working night and day for his sustenance, as well preaching the Gospel. He even called upon leaders: *"Follow my example, as I follow the example of Christ" (1 Corinthians 11:1).* But this is not the pattern that was seen in those African churches. Quite simply, lack of scriptural knowledge results in preachers engaging in ungodly activities, trying to serve God through ungodly means, and the results are dire.

Most of the people who left their jobs in mistaken response to the call of God suffered, and ended up begging from an already overloaded congregation. Most lost their faith, some backslid and some went back to work. The gospel of sowing and reaping money had not worked. It only brought pain, bitterness and resentment.

From such an era came a new breed of pastors, those who could manipulate people and the Word to suit what they wanted.

A story is told of one government minister who was worried about a church that pulled prospective graduates out of their jobs and into full-time ministry. They would have meetings every day of the week, and the politician confronted the church leaders and asked: "You attend church every day of the week, from Monday to Friday. Is your God going to rain down food from heaven for you? Is he going to rain down money for rent?" Sadly, he was chided as the devil's agent who did not understand faith, but he was right! The Bible agrees with what he said. As an unbeliever, he was wiser than the children of the kingdom. He understood the Genesis principle of working for your provision, while the church did not. Jesus Himself said that *"the children of this world are more shrewd in dealing with the world around them than are the children of the light" (Luke 16:8)*.

The government minister could see that there was no wisdom in attending church every day of the week and still expecting to prosper. The Thessalonians almost fell into the same problem, leading Paul to rebuke them. They were expecting an imminent return of Christ and in so doing ignored work and other important responsibilities as they thought Christ would come and take over, making their lives easy. See *2 Thessalonians 3:6-15*.

Chapter Ten

WORK IN CHRIST'S FIELDS - HARVESTING FOR GOD

I n *Matthew 6:33* Jesus teaches us to seek first the kingdom of God and His righteousness and then all our other needs will be taken care of. That may not mean that a bucket of wealth will be poured into our bank account while we just give and sow our offerings.

Jesus further teaches us to ask in order to receive, in *Mathew 7:7*. There is no mention of sowing anything in order for anybody to receive. And asking outside the will of God may not guarantee receiving, as indicated by *1 John 5:14*. It is also implied in *Matthew 20:20-24*, where the mother of Zebedee's children asks Jesus for positions of importance for her sons. Jesus tells her and her sons that they do not know what they are asking for. How often does that apply to us? We think our requests are genuine and warranted, yet in the eyes of God they are not. On the sons' insistence that they can drink the same 'cup' as Jesus, Jesus tells them that it is not in His power to grant their desire, because God grants such places *(verse 23)*. James calls this asking amiss.

The condition for receiving God's provision is to seek His kingdom and His righteousness. Righteousness refers to integrity, virtue, purity of life, rightness, and correctness of thinking, feeling and acting. It also refers in a narrower sense to justice, or the virtue which gives each his due. There is no abuse of another in righteousness; there is no deception. Righteousness involves the qualities that Paul talks about in the chapter on love in the book of Corinthians: *"love is never glad about injustice but rejoices whenever the truth wins out"* *(1 Corinthians 13:6)*. This is what we should seek.

Paul makes it clear what the kingdom of God is all about: *"For the kingdom of God is not a matter of eating and drinking, but of righteousness, peace and joy in the Holy Spirit"* *(Romans 14:17)*. The following verse says that if we serve God this way, we will please Him and be respected by people. Also, Paul writes in the book of Colossians: *"Since, then, you have been raised with Christ, set your hearts on things above, where Christ is seated at the right hand of God. Set your minds on things above, not on earthly things"* *(3:1-2)*.

The priority of many ministers of the Gospel needs to be set straight. Many give the appearance of seeking things that are above, but their hearts are far from that. People should be presented with the Gospel of Jesus, not the promise of prosperity. The Word tells us that God is a Spirit and that those who worship Him should do so in spirit and in truth

(John 4:24). Jesus also teaches us to concentrate on things that don't pass away, rather than on things of the world that do: *"Heaven and earth will pass away, but my words will never pass away" (Matthew 24:35).*

The world is prospering (materially) without admitting that there is a God. Why then would it take giving and sowing seed in offerings for the believer to prosper? Non-Christians work hard and prosper without a single prayer. Why then would Christians struggle in this area when we have the support of an Almighty God?

David observed this in *Psalm 73:3 (KJV): "For I was envious at the foolish, when I saw the prosperity of the wicked."* The wicked prosper yet they do not admit that there is a God. David calls them fools because they do not acknowledge God: *"The fool says in his heart, there is no God" (Psalm 14:1).* Yet David clearly admits that they prosper. This means that they know something that most believers do not know. If Solomon advised sluggards to go and learn from the ants *(Proverbs 6:6)*, I would suggest that, by the same token, we can enquire from those who are doing well, be they believers or not! They are still people and they have answers that might help us in our struggles.

This should make us Christians ashamed! What is it that the unbelievers are doing right that we are not? They are following the basic principles laid out in the Word, even though they do not realise it and don't even believe in God. The Bible, through James, instructs us to be doers of the Word, but most of us only do the aspects that we are comfortable doing.

Unbelievers work hard with their hands; they are diligent and most of them do give to the poor in their communities. They do the latter out of sheer goodness and compassion – they do not do it in order to prosper, because they are already prosperous. They never consider it sowing for a harvest, and that makes their attitude right when they give and that leads to blessing. In fact, it makes them less selfish than those Christians who give in order to get something back from God.

God honours anyone who honours His Word: that is the reason He causes the blessing of rain to fall on believers and unbelievers alike. He has not made hard work the key to the kingdom but it certainly is the way for us to be sustained, as He says in His Word. He is not a man that He should lie, and He never reverses what He has said in His Word. God does not concentrate on what passes away and He warns us not to place our trust in nor focus our lives on treasure that passes away. The wealth of the world can never be the focus of the kingdom. This is the reason the disciples had to leave it behind in order to attain the kingdom.

Give them to eat

My sister-in-law is a very active member of her church. She suggested that their church should celebrate a yearly event called the Harvest Festival. This involved every member of the congregation bringing either a bit of what they had harvested in the field or something they had bought that could be used for the day.

No one was excluded; even the poor were encouraged to contribute something. There was no promise of a blessing or anything financial in return. The idea was to have a festival where everybody participates and has something to eat and share. It was about sharing and fellowship.

Throughout the day the church engaged in programmes that promote unity and a communal spirit. The poor in the surrounding area were given free food to eat, as the Harvest Festival is a celebration of sharing resources. The remaining food was then donated to a nearby orphanage. They now do this every year!

When I asked her about the purpose of the event, she pointed me to one of the verses where the disciples wanted Jesus to provide food for the people and Jesus asked them to do it themselves: *"As evening approached, the disciples came to him and said, 'This is a remote place, and it's already getting late. Send the crowds away, so that they can go to the villages and buy themselves some food'"* (Matthew 14:15). Jesus' reply should make us think before we expect people to just give.

This was not the time to collect an offering or any of those spiritual things. The situation called for a practical solution. The disciples had nothing to offer and as a result wanted to throw the responsibility on Jesus. They wanted to off-load the 'monkey on their back' onto Jesus' back, but He refused and threw the challenge back to the disciples. *"You give them something to eat,"* was His reply *(verse 16).* While they were trying to calculate the money that would be needed to buy food, Jesus showed them that the kingdom was not about money but the power of God. This type of giving did not require any monetary transaction. We must not always view giving in the light of money.

Inspired by this Scripture, my sister-in-law started something that is now a yearly event and the community is being helped as everybody gives – not for a reward or a harvest, but out of a freely giving heart. This is what the Christian walk is about. Jesus did not place the responsibility of caring for one another on God. He placed it directly at the feet of the apostles and us, and He demonstrated how it should be done.

There are times when Jesus allowed the disciples to go and buy some food, as seen in *John 4:8.* He could have easily done the same. But in the feeding of the five thousand Jesus is showing us that the kingdom of God is not based on money all the time. This kind of giving does not require an offering bowl at all. We can do this within our communities as a sign of goodwill and godliness. Our minds must be liberated from the attitude of giving with the hope of getting more. It is unscriptural and it never works. According to *Matthew 6:1-4* the Pharisees were giving in order to receive the praises of men and it was wrong. Some of us give in order to get more and this is also wrong. Jesus warns us to take care or watch out when we give. In other words, what is our heart's attitude? If it's wrong, we will not be rewarded, according to verse one.

The silent giver

June 13th 2009 was a very sad day for us. It was the day we buried my father-in-law. What a wonderful man he was! He was a very simple and loving man, and as we quickly discovered that day, he was very much a giver and greatly impacted numerous lives in his community without us knowing what he was doing. None of us quite knew of these good works until crowds came that day to pay their last respects to their hero, whom I refer to as the silent giver.

There were so many testimonies from those he had touched through his generosity and those who were now wondering who would step in to help them. The community took the burial into their hands because of what he was to them. We never even had the opportunity to throw a single shovelful of soil to cover him as tradition requires.

The community that he so tirelessly served felt indebted to do everything because he had done so much for them. We understood them and allowed them the freedom they wanted.

He never sung songs of his good works; neither did he quote them Bible verses. He simply gave! For all his giving, he never expected anything back. He gave because he had something to give. He gave in order to improve the lives of others. He had something to give because he also received it from his children. He could have easily stored for a rainy day, but he never did.

He gave in various forms. For some he used his vehicle as a community ambulance; to others he gave clothing, and to some it was employment. There were reports of children he educated. Some had even become pastors because he had facilitated their training. There were numerous accounts of his good works. In all this, it was the receiver who benefited – not the giver.

It was truly more blessed to give than to receive, as the Lord Jesus said, and today those people take care of not just themselves but also the needy among them because they remember very well how they were helped by my father-in-law. This is the purpose of giving – to make a difference in the communities we live in. Not because we seek a greater harvest or prosperity, but because God's grace has been sufficient to enable us to have enough to give away. My father-in-law's funeral was packed with young people he had inspired, old people he had assisted, and a number of handicapped he never ignored. He was truly a giver, yet his giving was not an instrument for getting more for himself.

Jesus points out that a giver who seeks earthly rewards, whether in the form of material things or recognition, gets their temporal reward but loses their eternal one *(Matthew 6:2)*. This is what the Word says. The reward, though it could come in our lifetime, is not the focus: Jesus makes it clear that He will bring our reward for the good work that we do when He comes back *(Matthew 16:27)*.

Although he received support from his children, my father-in-law came out of retirement to continue working for an additional 14 years, just so that he could use his skill to help others. He prayed, yes, but he worked hard and used his rewards to give to those who could not make it on their own. No organisation worked with him, yet he did what many organisations fail to do with the support of many people.

Our giving should not only be limited to the church offering plate. The world is too broad and our eyes should be looking at what we can do to help the world around us.

Giving and fundraising

It is important to distinguish between giving and fundraising. For many churches today, this has been drawn under the same umbrella and similar Scriptures used to refer to both. This should not be so! The Wikipedia free encyclopaedia defines fundraising in the following words:

"Fundraising or fund raising is the process of soliciting and gathering contributions as money or other resources, by requesting donations from individuals, businesses, charitable foundations, or governmental agencies. Although fundraising typically refers to efforts to gather money for non-profit organizations, it is sometimes used to refer to the identification and solicitation of investors or other sources of capital for-profit [sic] enterprises."

It must be noted that fundraising is about soliciting money, which is why it is called fundraising. The term 'solicit' refers to begging, asking for, pleading for and petitioning for. This is what many Christian organisations and churches are doing today, especially Christian television programmes. They are begging for funds to keep their institutions afloat and they do so by requesting money from individuals. To request is to ask for or to demand. Begging is seen as shameful in the Bible, as it is against the promises of the blessing of God upon His people. In *Luke 16:3*, the manager says to himself: *"What shall I do now? My master is taking away my job… and I'm ashamed to beg…"* Begging was a shame. David actually listed it as a curse that he wished upon his enemies: *"May his children be wandering beggars; may they be driven from their ruined homes" (Psalm 109:10).*

Begging was not a good thing; it did not show the presence and the blessing of God. To remove the stigma attached to fundraising appeals, modern churches have termed it sowing. They literally implore or 'beg' people to sow and the promise is that they will reap a harvest. There is even a teaching that encourages people to sow more: *"Those who sow sparingly will reap sparingly" (2 Corinthians 9:6)* they will quote, so that under the guise of Scripture they don't appear to be begging.

The Bible is very practical about sowing and reaping, as we have already seen. In *Proverbs 20:4* the Bible teaches: *"The lazy man will not plow because of winter; he will beg during harvest and have nothing" (NKJV).* The ploughing comes before one can sow, and it's about breaking the land to prepare it for the next phase, that of sowing. The harvest has always been about that which has been worked. The fundraising harvest that comes with begging is definitely not for the benefit of those being begged to give.

In his book, 'Kings and Priests', David High makes a piercing observation: "Many good, godly men have destroyed themselves and their ministries when they felt they had to become fund-raisers. "Once they start chasing money, something twists inside and their message and ministry begins to ring hollow." How true! Paul also alluded to this when he warned Timothy about chasing money: *"People who want to get rich fall into temptation and a trap and into many foolish and harmful desires that plunge men into ruin and destruction. For the love of money is a root of all kinds of evil. Some people, eager for money, have wandered from the faith and pierced themselves with many griefs" (1 Timothy 6:9-10).* Paul then tells Timothy: *"But you, man of God, flee from all this" (verse 11).* Soliciting basically is driven by the solicitor, for his purposes. He is the one in need and takes a step to gratify that need.

Giving, on the other hand, is different; it emanates from the giver, who sees a need and willingly chooses to meet it without any pressure, although this can sometimes be in response to the pleading of a solicitor. In Exodus, God told Moses that the people were to give willingly: *"The Lord said to Moses, 'Tell the Israelites to bring me an offering. You are to receive the offering for me from each man whose heart prompts him to give" (Exodus 25:1-2).*

The Wikipedia defines giving in the sense that what is given is a gift, and a gift or a present is the transfer of something

141

without the need for compensation that is involved in trade. A gift is a voluntary act which does not require anything in return. Even though it involves possibly a social expectation of reciprocity, or a return in the form of prestige or power, a gift is meant to be free.

If an ordinary layman's understanding of giving is so clear, one wonders why the Church of Jesus Christ puts so much confusion into the message of giving. There should be no expectation of any return in what we give. We must not be taught to expect a harvest after we give. It's only a way of indirectly forcing people to give in to the pleas of leaders of ministries who have ambitions and agendas.

What then shall we do?

The purpose of the Gospel must be clear each time it is preached. This purpose is derived from the reason why God sent Jesus to this world. The message to Joseph by Gabriel the great angel was: *"She will give birth to a son, and you are to give him the name Jesus, because he will save his people from their sins" (Matthew 1:21).* This is the purpose of the Gospel: to bring repentance from a life of unrighteousness to a life of godliness.

This message was clear from Jesus' own ministry. In *Matthew 4:17* we are told: *"From that time on Jesus began to preach, 'Repent, for the kingdom of heaven is near.'"* Peter is no different, as can be seen after his first sermon in the book of Acts: *"When the people heard this, they were cut to the heart and said to Peter and the other apostles, 'Brothers, what shall we do?"' (Acts 2:37).* The reply emulates Jesus and the words are similar. In *verse 38* Peter says to them: *"Repent and be baptised, every one of you, in the name of Jesus Christ for the forgiveness of your sins. And you will receive the gift of the Holy Spirit."* Two issues stand out in Peter's reply: repentance and forgiveness of sins. These issues were also highlighted in the teachings of John the Baptist and the apostle Paul. People are rarely given a chance to ask this question these days, yet it is the most important question for those who have heard the Gospel. They need to know how to respond to the Gospel message.

Watching many preachers on the television these days makes the Gospel a joke. People are not even given the opportunity to ask the question, let alone to respond to the Word in repentance. Most sermons end with the collection of an offering. Why? Where is this spirit coming from? I believe many preachers have now been desensitised and the love and pursuit of money has gripped them.

Conferences and TV programmes are now run as fundraising platforms. After a wonderful sermon and teaching, when people are supposed to clean up their hearts through prayer and repentance, the preacher finds it a good opportunity to collect a big offering, while peoples' hearts are tender. The preacher even tells them what to do after he has spoken, because he knows that they are asking a question: "What should I do now?" His quick suggestion that people give an offering ends the opportunity to repent because the offering replaces that need and response. This is the reason why many

143

people find it easier to go and drop an offering at the altar when the Word of God pierces them during the preaching, than to repent – and the preacher is not stopping them. Hence there is no growth and depth in the people, as what should be dealt with as heart issues are now resolved and dealt with through the power of money.

The Word will always convict us of our sin. It is the job of the minister to then lead people to the cross to get repentance. Leading them to the offering bowl sends the message that they need to buy their salvation, when really, Jesus has already paid the price.

Some may argue that we cannot be receiving repentance every time the Word is preached; it's just not practical. That is a good point, but the Word is clear again on this. Paul tells us that some of his teachings are given so that Christ can be formed in us. In *Galatians 4:19* he says: *"My dear children, for whom I am again in the pains of childbirth until Christ is formed in you..."*

The formation process is long and takes place each time the Word is preached. It also requires a spiritual response, considering the fact that God is a spirit and that which is born is a spiritual thing. The word 'formed' is the Greek 'morphoo', meaning 'to form', and it relates to an eternal reality. When Paul uses it in *Galatians 4:19*, it is referring to a change in character, becoming conformed to the character of Christ in actuality, not merely a superficial resemblance.

This is supported by *Romans chapter 12:2: "Do not be conformed to this world, but be transformed by the renewing of your mind, that you may prove what is that good and acceptable and perfect will of God" (NKJV)*. This conformation to the world is the opposite of the formation of Christ in us, and it is constantly bombarded by the preaching of the Word.

To 'conform' is derived from the Greek 'suchematizo', which refers to accommodating oneself to a model or pattern, which is the lusts of this world according to *1 Peter 1:14*. Whenever the Word is preached to believers, the aim is to consolidate the repentance they have made and to help them renew their minds in order to maintain the character of Christ that is slowly developing inside them. It all requires a spiritual response. And the listeners will always ask, "What shall we do?"

The renewal of the mind therefore speaks of Godliness and moral purity, which is what Jesus brought. We must realise that the mind constitutes the intellect or understanding, but also includes everything that is described in the word 'mindset' (what you set your mind on), that is the feelings and the will. Being transformed by the renewing of the mind indicates a literal change in the form of thought after being stimulated by the Word, in this case.

This process describes the provision that Christ makes in redemption and the power it has through the Holy Spirit to instil Godliness in our thoughts, which leads to the formulating of our purpose, which in turn dictates our actions, which in turn shapes our character by determining our habits. The path of holiness is a life that consistently requires the direction of the Word and that is the reason preachers should be preaching and calling for repentance.

People must not be denied the opportunity to ask this most important question. In fact, preachers should by now know that this question always follows their preaching and simply facilitate that repentance, rather than beginning with an offering.

Paul, when faced with a similar situation, quickly brought order and refused a carnal response to a spiritual question. After performing a miracle at Lystra, Paul was faced with the possibility of a carnal response: *"The priest of Zeus… brought bulls and wreaths to the city gates because he and the crowd wanted to offer sacrifices to them [Paul and Barnabas]"* *(Acts 14:13).* When Paul and Barnabas heard this, the Word tells us that they tore their clothes in protest and refused to receive a sacrifice because it implied they were taking the place of God. Their humility was clear: *"We too are only men, human like you"* was their contention *(verse 15).* It is so easy to be carried away when God is doing great things through us and we must be careful of that.

Conclusion

Giving is vital because it confirms and consolidates our faith in God, according to James. He calls giving the outworking of faith or the evidence of the presence of God in one's life. Faith without these works is dead, in his view. He derives this from a challenge he gives us in his book about how we should respond to the needs of people around us: *"Suppose a brother or sister is without clothes and daily food. If one of you says to him, 'Go, I wish you well; keep warm and well fed,' but does nothing about his physical needs, what good is it?" (James 2:15-16).*

James further postulates that Abraham, the father of faith, was actually justified by his action of giving his son Isaac for sacrifice in obedience to God's instruction. *"You see that his faith and his actions were working together, and his faith was made complete by what he did" (2:22).* Giving makes our faith active and complete or practical.

This makes giving a critical and very important part of any believer's faith, as "good works" was one of the evidences of the anointing upon Jesus Christ, according to *Acts 10:37-38: "You know what has happened... how God anointed Jesus of Nazareth with the Holy Spirit and power, and how he went around doing good...."* And He commanded us to do the works that He did, and even more. We cannot therefore use our giving as bait to get more wealth, which would be a travesty against the nature and character of God and the purpose of the Scriptures.

Work and giving are two distinct principles that yield totally different results. I work and I get paid; I give and I lose what I got paid. This is the essence of giving. We don't give as a seed to gain more – we gain more through our work or jobs. Through the process of working, what I lose is my energy, but this results in wages that add to my wealth. Giving, however, takes away the wealth that I have made through work. That is the reason why giving is both a choice and a command. Work causes an inflow into my life, while giving results in an outflow. One multiplies and the other takes away. That is the reason why giving is difficult for some people.

It is not easy to give unless you have been taught from an early age to share. No wonder many people teach that you get a big harvest when you give, and this then releases more people to give because of the hope of making more. This simply means that without the promise of a harvest, many people would find it difficult to freely give. This is precisely the reason why many preachers teach that you get most when what you give pains you. If you don't feel pain when you give, then you have not truly given. This couldn't be further from the truth. There is no Scriptural basis to it other than the fact that you have not given willingly and you are not a cheerful giver – period.

Why must pain be related to giving? Pain is an indication of a problem not a joy. When I give grumbling, I have still given; when I give cursing, I have still given. The only difference is that I have not done it willingly, thus the grumbling. The Bible advises us not to give if we do it grudgingly. It does not help the one receiving when it is done with grudges.

I used to have a sister who would throw things at me whenever she gave me something. It was hurtful and I only received because I was desperate. She was not a willing giver. She gave because she had to. I still remember her meanness, even now, long after she died.

The reason for our giving is to do good to the recipient. God actually pays attention to our giving and our attitude towards giving, as shown in the story of the widow and her two mites. We cannot afford to underestimate the principles and practices of giving or take it lightly as Christians, despite the wrong teachings on it. It is still the back bone of the life of a believer who now has the nature of God in him, and that very God is a giver.

The story of Cornelius sheds light on this concept. The Bible tells us that this man was devout, meaning he was dedicated to God – which is what every believer should be. According to *Acts 10*, he feared God and this commitment and reverence for God made him a generous giver and a prayerful man. What a combination for blessings. God showed him an angel in a vision, and the angel commented on his giving and actually stated that his giving had caught the attention of God.

God does pay attention to our giving and this makes giving an important aspect of our faith. I don't believe that Cornelius gave in order to reap a harvest or to get more. He gave because he had the heart of God; no wonder he is described as a devout and God-fearing man. This is the practice that every believer should be emulating. God did not tell him about a harvest but sent something better in His judgement – an experience of salvation for his entire household.

Why was God attracted to Cornelius' giving? Because he had faith and his faith was shown through his works of giving and praying. As James says, *faith without works is dead (James 2:20)*, and we can only show that we have faith when we reflect the works of faith through our giving to those in need. This is important, because Scripture also tells us that faith pleases God and giving is part of our faith. God is pleased when we give. Without faith, we are taught in the Scriptures, it is impossible to please God *(Hebrews 11:6)*. Giving is intrinsic to faith, so I think we are safe to say that without giving it is impossible to please God.

The important thing, though, is our attitude as we give. We should be giving because we love. We love because we have God inside us, and God is love and His love does not fail, it does not give up and it does not insist on its own ways. Love is good, and goodness is a character trait that Jesus specifically attributed to God. The anointing, according to Acts 10:38, enabled Jesus to go about doing good, and most of this good was giving to those in need – be it healing, wine at a wedding, honour and dignity (as in the case of a woman found in adultery), freedom from demons (as in the case of Mary Magdalene), opening of blind eyes, and finally, the forgiveness of the sins of the world. Jesus always gave, and He gave us His mission. He said: *"As the Father has sent Me, I also send you" (John 20:21, NJKV).* He has given us His identity and His power through the Holy Spirit. Jesus is indeed a giver, and all that for no expectation at all.

Give and give and continue to give as you see the need: it is more blessed to give than to receive. And remember you do not do it because you want something out of it; it is merely evidence that you have faith and that the Son of God is living in you.

We, as disciples of Christ, are called to live as Christ lived. That is mostly demonstrated through our acts of kindness and good works, through our responses to the needs of the world we live in, as James points out. The character of a faithful servant is revealed in his devotion to the interests of others and his thoughtfulness of extending a helping hand, giving a gift and the mere joy in meeting the needs of the less fortunate. All these opportunities to give should be grasped by believers. The Bible teaches us that to delight in the prosperity, honour and even the happiness of another is a reflection of the heart of a Christian.

Giving must be voluntary and it is motivated from within by the love of God, who now inhabits our hearts. It must never be imposed; it is not mandated by needs or insistence or manipulation by a third party. There must be no pressure or guilt when we cannot give. It must always be done in the Spirit of Christ who gave His life for the world. If this is how we approach our acts of kindness and goodwill, the world will be a better place. We must be determined to make a difference by releasing what we have to better others. If God wants you to give something, He will not go via another person to tell you what to give. He is right inside you and should easily speak to you. It is okay for people to make appeals, but that should not put anyone under pressure as God does not pressurise us into doing anything. He leads us like a good shepherd.

All this said, we must not forget that the Bible does promise rewards to those who obey the instructions recorded in it. Jesus actually promised that on His return He would be coming with a reward for all who perform good works: "Behold, I am coming soon! My reward is with me, and I will give to everyone according to what he has done" *(Revelation 22:12)*. He says something similar in *Matthew 5:12: "Rejoice and be glad, because great is your reward in heaven...."* There definitely is a reward for good works and this further confirms the goodness of God: even at the end of time He is still giving.

REFERENCES

Chapter One

1. www.brainyquote.com/quotes/authors/d/david/_rockerfeller.html

2. www.brainyquote.com/quotes/authors/m/maya_angelou.html

Chapter Two

1. www.markswatson.com/sikes1.htm
2. www.markswatson.com/sikes1.htm
3. www.markswatson.com/sikes1.htm

Chapter Three

1. Terrance Irwin, Dissertation, Examining God's Will for Christians with Regard to Prosperity, 2007

2. Stephen R Covey, The 7 Habits of Highly Effective People, CPI Mackays, Catham, 1989, pp18-24

3. Covey, p.184

4. Covey, p. 18-19

5. Covey, p. 21-22

6. Covey, p. 21

7. Covey, p. 22

8. Terrance Irwin, Dissertation, Examining God's Will for Christians with Regard to Prosperity, 2007

9. John Wesley quoted in Charles Edward White, 'Four Lessons on Money from One of the World's Richest Preachers', Christian History 19 (Summer 1998), p. 21-22

10. Randy Alcorn, Money Possessions and Eternity, Tyndale House Publishers, Inc., 2003, p. 448

11. Alcorn, p. 248

12. Covey, p. 74

Chapter Five

1. Mark A. Snoeberger, The Pre-Mosaic Tithe: Issues and Implications, Detroit Baptist Seminary Journal 5 (Fall 2000): p. 71-95, Internet accessed, 09/04/08

2. JBF Commentary, p. 30-31

3. Neil Chadwick, Giving and Receiving, 8th Day Pastoral Reflection, 26/12/04, Orthodox Mission, USA

4. The King James Bible Commentary, Thomas Nelson: Nashville, 1997, p. 1994

5. The King James Bible Commentary, Thomas Nelson: Nashville, 1997, p. 1994

6. Matthew Henry, Matthew Henry's Commentary on the whole Bible: Hendrickson: Peabody

7. Ernest L. Martin, The Tithing Dilemma Portland, Associates for Scriptural Knowledge, 197, p.22

8. Murray, Beyond Tithing, p.70

9. William R. Cunningham, Tithing, Giving, Sowing and Reaping Journal, Version 2, June 1998

Chapter Six

1. Oral Roberts, Miracle Seed Faith, Tulsa, Oral Roberts Association, 1992, p. 25

2. Ilumina Encyclopedia, www.tyndale.com

3. Matthew Henry, p. 132

4. Jamieson, Fausset and Brown, JFB Commentary, A Practical Commentary on the Whole Bible, Grand Rapids, Zondervan Publishing House, 1962, p. 73

5. Christian History Magazine, Volume VI, Number 2, Christian History Institute, 1987, p. 4

6. Ibid, p.4

7. T. Miles, Malachi, The Broadman Bible Commentary, Volume 7; Clifton J. Allen, Nashville: Broadman, 1972, p. 390

8. Jacob Milgrom, Numbers, The JPS Torah Commentary, Philadelphia: Jewish Publication Society, 1990

9. John MacArthur Jr. God's Plan for Giving, Chicago, Moody Press, 1982, p. 76

10. Peter Wade, http://www.peterwade.com, internet accessed: 20/03/08

10. Peter Wade, http://www.peterwade.com, internet accessed: 20/03/08

Chapter Seven

1. Jim Davis, Giving Generously Journal

2. Craig L.Bloomberg, Interpreting the Parables, Downer's Grove, Inter-Varsity Press, 1990, p. 257-258.

Chapter Nine

1. H. Bushnell, Ralph Cushman, The New Christian: Studies in Christian Stewardship, Centenary Conservation Committee – Methodist Episcopal Church, 1991, p.39, 132

2. S. M. Houghton, Sketches of Pentecostal Church History, The Bath Press, 1980, p. 8

3. Hudson Taylor, Money, Possessions and Eternity, p. 252

Chapter Ten

1. David High, Kings and Priests, Oklahoma City: Books for Children of the World, 1997, p. 26, 28

OTHER BOOKS BY SIBANDA PUBLISHING

Woman! You are God s special gift to the world. Deposited within you is a unique and valuable fragrance waiting to be released. Regardless of how you started in life, the experiences you have been through or the challenges you may be currently facing, God has great plans for you. Don t allow anything or anyone to reduce you to something God never intended you to be. This book will equip and empower you to let go of your past, walk in your present and embrace your future. You can rise up, release your godly fragrance and make a difference in this world!

For more information please contact info@sibandapublishing.com